"Walter Brueggemann is a legend. He is  biblical scholars of the past century. Fev  more than Brueggemann, especially as \  it means to be God's peculiar people in ... ueny or the empire. This series is sort of like the 'best hits' album of one of the world's greatest theologians."

—Shane Claiborne, author, activist,  and cofounder of Red Letter Christians

"Do not miss the opportunity to use this powerful resource to spur life-changing conversation among people of faith. We are living in a moment when scarcity seduces us, permitting us to cling to our privilege and rendering us unable to see how the narrative of scarcity harms not just us but the neighbors we are called to care for. Here Brueggemann offers us the text and the witness of our faith to insist that we reject the fear and despair around us and tenaciously embrace the abundance and grace by which people of faith are invited and called by God to move through this world. This is a treasure!"

—Amy Butler, founder of Invested Faith  and author of *Beautiful and Terrible Things*

"If you have about had it with the Bible or if you preach to people who feel the Bible does more harm than good, Walter Brueggemann's *Grace Abounds* is the medicine you need. It rescues us from the all-too-common and all-too-shallow ways the Bible is typically quoted and wielded like a weapon; it gently leads us down into the Bible's deepest currents—currents that challenge many of our most deeply held paradigms and ultimately liberate us from them. I am among those for whom Walter Brueggemann has saved the Bible and shown us what it is really for. Don't miss *Grace Abounds*."

—Brian D. McLaren, author of  *Do I Stay Christian?* and *Life after Doom*

"With profound biblical insight and sensitivity to the needs of the world, Walter Brueggemann reminds us why his voice is one of the most important pastoral voices of this generation. In *Grace*

*Abounds*, we are reintroduced to an imagination offering the abundance of grace even in the most broken of worlds."

—Soong-Chan Rah, author of *Prophetic Lament*
and Robert Boyd Munger Professor of Evangelism and
Church Renewal, Fuller Theological Seminary

"This book is a biblical witness to the fullness of life. Brueggemann has gifted us with an antidote to many sins of our present economy. *Grace Abounds* offers people of faith a way forward and an invitation to take part in the still unfolding story of God's creative abundance."

—Erin Wathen, pastor of Grace Immanuel United
Church of Christ and author of *Resist and Persist*

# Grace Abounds

# Grace Abounds

## God's Abundance against the Fear of Scarcity

*Walter Brueggemann*

WESTMINSTER
JOHN KNOX PRESS
LOUISVILLE · KENTUCKY

*First edition*
Published by Westminster John Knox Press
Louisville, Kentucky

24 25 26 27 28 29 30 31 32 33—10 9 8 7 6 5 4 3 2 1

Unless otherwise indicated, Scripture quotations are from the New Revised Standard Version of the Bible, copyright © 1989 by the Division of Christian Education of the National Council of the Churches of Christ in the U.S.A., and are used by permission.

See acknowledgments, pp. 145–46, for additional permission.

*Book design by Sharon Adams*
*Cover design by designpointinc.com*

Library of Congress Cataloging-in-Publication Data is on file
at the Library of Congress, Washington, DC.

ISBN: 978-0-664-26591-5 (paperback)
ISBN: 978-1-646-98409-1 (ebook)

Most Westminster John Knox Press books are available at special quantity discounts when purchased in bulk by corporations, organizations, and special-interest groups. For more information, please email SpecialSales@wjkbooks.com.

*We happily dedicate this volume to our partners,*
*Tia Brueggemann and Stephanie Hankins,*
*who amaze us with both grace abundant and love profound.*

# Contents

# Series Preface

*I* have been very pleased that David Dobson and his staff at Westminster John Knox Press have proposed this extended series of republications of my work. Indeed, I know of no old person who is not pleased to be taken seriously in old age! My first thought, in learning of this proposed series, is that my life and my work have been providentially fortunate in having good companions all along the way who have both supported me and for the most part kept me honest in my work. I have been blessed by the best teachers, who have prepared me to think both critically and generatively. I have been fortunate to be accompanied by good colleagues, both academic and pastoral, who have engaged my work. And I have been gifted to have uncommonly able students, some of whom continue to instruct me in the high art of Old Testament study.

The long years of my work that will be represented in this series reflect my slow process of finding my own voice, of sorting out accents and emphases, and of centering my work on recurring themes that I have judged to merit continuing attention. The result of that slow process is that over time my work is marked by repetition and reiteration, as well as contradiction, change of mind, and ambiguity, all of which belong to seeing my work as an organic whole as I have been given courage and insight. In the end I have settled on recurring themes (reflected in the organization of this series) that I hope I have continued to treat with imagination, so that my return to them is not simply reiteration but is critically generative of new perspective and possibility.

In retrospect I can identify two learnings from the philosopher and hermeneut Paul Ricoeur that illumine my work. Ricoeur has given me names for what I have been doing, even though I was at work on such matters before I acquired Ricoeur's terminology. First, in his book *Freud and Philosophy* (1965), Ricoeur identifies two moves that are essential for interpretation. On the one hand there is "suspicion." By this term Ricoeur means critical skepticism. In biblical study "suspicion" has taken the form of historical criticism in which the interpreter doubts the "fictive" location and function of the text and hypothesizes about the "real, historical" location and function of the text. On the other hand there is "retrieval," by which Ricoeur means the capacity to reclaim what is true in the text after due "suspicion." My own work has included measures of "suspicion," because a grounding in historical criticism has been indispensable for responsible interpretation. My work, however, is very much and increasingly tilted toward "retrieval," the recovery of what is theologically urgent in the text. My own location in a liberal-progressive trajectory of interpretation has led me to an awareness that liberal-progressives are tempted to discard "the baby" along with "the bath." For that reason my work has been to recover and reclaim, I hope in generative imaginative ways, the claims of biblical faith.

Second and closely related, Ricoeur has often worked with a grid of "precritical/critical/postcritical" interpretation. My own schooling and that of my companions has been in a critical tradition; that enterprise by itself, however, has left the church with little to preach, teach, or trust. For that reason my work has become increasingly postcritical, that is, with a "second naiveté," a readiness to engage in serious ways the claims of the text. I have done so in a conviction that the alternative metanarratives available to us are inadequate and the core claims of the Bible are more adequate for a life of responsible well-being. Both liberal-progressive Christians and fundamentalist Christians are tempted and seduced by alternative narratives that are elementally inimical to the claims of the Bible; for that reason the work of a generative exposition of biblical claims seems to me urgent. Thus I anticipate that this series may be a continuing invitation to the ongoing urgent work of exposition that both makes clear the singular claims of the Bible and exposes the inadequacy of competing narratives that, from a biblical perspective, amount to idolatry. It is my hope that such continuing work will not only give preachers something substantive to preach and give teachers something substantive to teach, but will invite the church to embrace the biblical claims that it can "trust and obey."

My work has been consistently in response to the several unfolding crises facing our society and, more particularly, the crises faced by the church. Strong market forces and ideological passions that occupy center stage among us sore tempt the church to skew its tradition, to compromise its gospel claim, and to want to be "like the nations" (see 1 Sam. 8:5, 20), that is, without the embarrassment of gospel disjunction. Consequently I have concluded, over time, that our interpretive work must be more radical in its awareness that the claims of faith increasingly contradict the dominant ideologies of our time. That increasing awareness of contradiction is ill-served by progressive-liberal accommodation to capitalist interests or, conversely, it is ill-served by the packaged reductions of reactionary conservatism. The work we have now to do is more complex and more demanding than either progressive-liberal or reactionary-conservative offers. Thus our work is to continue to probe this normative tradition that is entrusted to us that is elusive in its articulation and that hosts a Holy Agent who runs beyond our explanatory categories in irascible freedom and in bottomless fidelity.

I am grateful to the folk at Westminster John Knox and to a host of colleagues who continue to engage my work. I am profoundly grateful to Davis Hankins, on the one hand, for his willingness to do the arduous work of editing this series. On the other hand, I am grateful to Davis for being my conversation partner over time in ways that have evoked some of my better work and that have fueled my imagination in fresh directions. I dare anticipate that this coming series of republication will, in generative ways beyond my ken, continue to engage a rising generation of interpreters in bold, courageous, and glad obedience.

Walter Brueggemann

# Editor's Introduction

$I$ began theological education just as Walter Brueggemann was scheduled to retire at Columbia Theological Seminary. I knew very little about the academic study of religion, probably even less about the state of biblical scholarship at the turn of the twenty-first century, yet somehow I knew enough to take every possible course with Dr. Brueggemann. After retiring, Walter continued to teach a course periodically and work from his study on campus—and he always insisted that it and any pastor's work space be called a "study" rather than an "office"! But before he retired, during his last and my first year at Columbia, I took six different courses in biblical studies, including three with Walter. In my memory, I spent that academic year much like St. Thecla as she sat in a windowsill and listened to the teachings of the apostle Paul. According to her mother's descriptive flourish, Thecla, "clinging to the window like a spider, lays hold of what is said by him with a strange eagerness and fearful emotion." It was for me as it had been for Thecla. I imagine my mother would empathize with hers.

Longtime readers as well as those encountering Walter's words for the first time will discover in the volumes of the Walter Brueggemann Library the same soaring rhetoric, engaging intelligence, acute social analysis, moral clarity, wit, generosity, and grace that make it so enlightening and enjoyable to learn from and with Walter Brueggemann. The world we inhabit is broken, dominated by the special interests of the wealthy, teeming with misinformation, divided by entrenched social hierarchies, often despairing before looming ecological catastrophe, and callously indifferent, if not aggressively predatory, toward those facing increasing deprivation and immiseration.

In these volumes readers will find Walter at his best, sharply naming these dynamics of brokenness and richly engaging biblical traditions to uncover and chart alternative forms of collective life that promise to be more just, more merciful, and more loving.

Each volume in the Walter Brueggemann Library coheres around a distinct theme that is a prominent concern across Walter's many publications. The contents of the volumes consist of materials taken from a variety of his previously published works. In other words, I have compiled whole chapters or articles, sections, snippets for some volumes, and at times even just a line or two from Walter's publications, and sought to weave them together to create a new book that coheres around a specific theme, in this case the theme of grace in the Bible.

Grace is one of the key terms associated with God and God's covenantal relationship with human communities in the Bible. In what many consider the most succinct and fundamental characterization of Israel's God in the Hebrew Bible, Exodus 34:6–7 offers a series of descriptors of core aspects of YHWH's identity, beginning with "merciful and gracious."[1] These and other adjectives used in these verses to describe YHWH (e.g., "patient," "faithful," "true") appear in numerous other texts in Scripture, attesting to a variety of ways that Israel understood grace and graciousness as central to YHWH's identity.[2] This particular passage occurs at a pivotal moment in Exodus and in Israel's life. Israel has only barely averted God's wrathful intent to destroy the people after the golden calf debacle (Exod. 32:1–10). As Brueggemann recounts, "In 32:11–14 and 33:12–16, Moses intercedes with Yahweh on behalf of Israel, parrying with Yahweh. Moses insists that Yahweh must go with Israel into the wilderness if there is to be any Israel. In response, Yahweh assures Moses that Yahweh is marked by profound and free graciousness, and will act graciously according to Yahweh's own free inclination."[3] These two verses in Exodus 34:6–7, describing God as both "abounding in steadfast love" and "yet by no means clearing the guilty," and the larger story in which they occur reveal a profound tension at the heart of the biblical God. On one hand, YHWH is committed to justice, to holding people accountable for their deeds by punishment for iniquity, breach of contract, and so on. On the other hand, YHWH is disposed to be merciful, gracious, and forgiving. The tension between these two commitments gets resolved in a variety of ways throughout the biblical texts, oftentimes in favor of the positive, merciful side. At other times that disposition gets overruled by the second half of the statement attesting to God's judgment and refusal to acquit the guilty. In many texts, this tension is unresolved but used by Israel to try to move YHWH toward one side or the other, or to criticize the Deity for favoring or neglecting one or the other.

Although these two characteristics of the Deity are not finally harmonized or settled in this Exodus passage or anywhere else in the Bible, they are described as unequal, both here and elsewhere.[4] God's gracious mercy is said to be exponentially greater—"for the thousandth generation"—than God's desire to punish iniquity—"to the third and the fourth generation." It is in this and other ways, as the chapters in this volume demonstrate, that the Bible associates God's grace with abundance. Further, Brueggemann urges, the Bible opposes God's abundant grace to various forms of scarcity as often as, if not more than, it does to punitive judgment. Throughout Scripture, God's actions are overwhelmingly tipped toward compassion and a desire to offer abundant life and liberation in concrete ways. For this reason, scarcity and abundance constitute the most important opposition in this volume on grace in the Bible.

The tension between abundance and scarcity is also important in these essays because of their contemporary relevance. We are bombarded in all kinds of different ways with the message and assumption that scarce resources are the prevailing condition of our lives.[5] Because there are only so many open jobs, a certain number of people seeking work must remain unemployed; because there is a limited quantity of natural resources, we must make every possible effort to maximize productivity; because there are fluctuations in the limited demand and supply of various goods and services, their costs rise or fall in economic markets; because the budget, the food supply, access to housing, and so forth, are limited, markets continue to function and do not collapse. A scarcity mind-set also links us together, albeit negatively, through the idea that because something is limited, someone else's access to or enjoyment of that thing may come at the cost of our own access or ability to enjoy it. Thus, we are bound together in contemporary society by, among other things, the negative connections created by seemingly endless circuits of competition and envy.

In much of today's society, abundance is the ostensible goal of our labor. On the premise of scarce resources, the often unstated but prevailing promise is that if we all work as hard as we can to produce as much as we can—striving in the meantime to secure whatever we can—then we can create enough to overcome the scarcity that drives our need to produce so much in the first place. But that promise can never be realized under capitalism. Consider how often economists and other partisans worry about abundance triggering price inflation, loss in productivity, reduction in consumption, declining investments, and so on. We cannot, many fear, raise the minimum wage or expand access to basic social services, because such abundance would discourage productivity, disrupt prices, decrease consumption, and so on. In short, our economy presupposes a belief in scarcity, encourages economic activities that pursue abundance, and yet cannot permit such an abundance to become a reality.

Abundance in the Bible interrupts and overcomes situations in which resources are scarce, but abundance does not function in the same way as the prevailing fantasy of an abundance that would eliminate scarcity and satisfy all desires. Biblical abundance, bestowed characteristically by a gracious God, undermines the presupposition of scarce resources but does not thereby pretend also to overcome the psychic investment in and social role played by scarcity. The wilderness is the characteristic place of scarcity in the Bible, and the paradigmatic biblical stories of abundance undermining the presupposition of scarcity are about God's provision of bread, quail, and water in that desert environment. God graciously provides all that the people need, but this does not prevent them from desiring something else to eat (see, e.g., Num. 11:4–5), from feeling envy of others (see, e.g., Num. 16:3), from complaining about the food that God provides (see, e.g., Num. 11:6), and from trying to hoard those very same provisions (see, e.g., Exod. 16:19–20). The Bible clearly understands that abundance is not mutually exclusive with scarcity, and it illustrates the psychic appeal of scarcity. Even when presented with abundance, many of us prefer to retreat into a scarcity mind-set. A scarcity mind-set is attractive because it implies that the reason for our dissatisfaction is not internal but external. A scarcity mind-set also offers a social bond with others who view their dissatisfaction as a result of their lack of something external, an idea that is often accompanied by the thought that someone else has whatever we lack. In other words, scarcity is appealing for all of the reasons why we may find a politics of envy seductive. The wilderness stories critique such a retreat into a scarcity mind-set, and, in holding up a mirror to show how we externalize our inner conflicts, encourage us to form social bonds on the basis of abundance rather than competition over scarce resources, which would make us much less susceptible to anxiety, envy, hoarding, and violence. This may be the most urgent lesson for us who inhabit this world of manufactured scarcity.

This book is divided into two parts. The first five chapters in part 1 lay out some fundamentals of biblical grace. Like Maslow with his hierarchy, Brueggemann begins in these five chapters with our most basic needs. Chapters 1 and 2, the longest chapters in the book, focus on our need to eat and metabolize food. Starting with an exploration of scarcity in chapter 1 and of abundance in chapter 2, Brueggemann appropriately frames these two conflicting perspectives under the rubric of a food fight. Chapter 3 turns to consider the land, who has access to it and rights over it, and how it is used. This provides a fitting transition from considerations of food in chapters 1 and 2 to the focus in chapter 4 on shelter, another of our most elemental needs. Brueggemann demonstrates that the Bible has much to say about housing crises and people experiencing homelessness, and he makes the case that the Bible advocates for "the practice of homefulness" in the face of and in contrast to manifestations of homelessness in our time, intensified by societal neglect. Finally, chapter 5 considers four different types of responses he finds from people in biblical texts struggling to live through experiences of radical displacement, such as exile and forced migration—responses that in different ways made it possible for ancient Israel to experience God's grace even in dire circumstances.

The five chapters in part 2 identify and advocate for specific biblical practices that are appropriate to the reality and experience of God's grace and grace-full relationships with fellow creatures and all creation. These five chapters commend, respectively, keeping Sabbath, making doxology, bestowing blessing, offering forgiveness, and realizing reconciliation. These five practices are not presented as an exhaustive list, but rather as a starting point for thinking about how we might respond bodily and in community to all that the Bible teaches about grace and God's graciousness in particular.

As I suggest in the discussion of abundance above, I think that grace-as-abundance can be difficult to receive. In fact, I think that for many of us it can be unnerving, perhaps even traumatic. Grace interrupts or suspends our usual ideas about what is appropriate, deserved, ethical. This is one reason why many of us may be quick to retreat from opportunities for and experiences of grace, following the temptation to turn from abundance to adopt a mind-set of scarcity. Grace is unnerving and unpredictable, in part because it creates new possibilities for human relationships and experiences that were not previously anticipated, and because it does not determine but rather opens new possibilities for how we might respond, which can give rise to a certain kind of anxiety. Thus I hope that the reflections on grace in this book will discourage us from retreating into anxiety over uncertainty, will make us more receptive to experiences of grace and more likely to pursue opportunities to be gracious, and will entangle us more deeply in grace-full relationships among ourselves and with all creation.

Finally, I want to thank everyone at Westminster John Knox for their support, encouragement, and wisdom in publishing this volume and the entire series, especially Julie Mullins, Julie Tonini, and David Dobson. Thanks also to Julie Hester for the care with which she composed the reflection questions at the end of each chapter in this volume. Although they do not all know it, I am profoundly aware that the support and friendship of many have helped this book see the light of day, including Francis Landy and all participants in the shiur hosted by Congregation Emanu-El in Victoria, British Columbia, as well as many other brilliant and hilarious friends, such as Brennan Breed, Sean Burt, Kelly Murphy, Brent Strawn, Elaine James, Kevin Schilbrack, Joe Weiss, Rick Elmore, Dief Alexander, Rhiannon Graybill, Mark Lewis, Tod Linafelt, and Tim Beal. By now I am fully aware that I will never repay Walter Brueggemann for the love and support that he has shown to me and my family for decades. Happily, I am pleased to live with that immense debt of gratitude all my days. Together Walter and I are honored to dedicate this volume to our spouses, who have proven to be consistent sources of abundant grace in our lives. A big heartfelt thank you to Tia and to Stephanie!

Davis Hankins
Appalachian State University
Spring 2024

# PART ONE

# Fundamentals of Biblical Grace

Chapter 1

# Food Fight I

Scarcity, Anxiety, Accumulation, and Monopoly

### Monopoly: Accountability for the Food Fight

The hunger crisis and food insecurity that so many face may lead one to believe that resources must be scarce, limited, and insufficient. The Bible, however, repeatedly tells stories of God graciously providing abundance that overcomes the threat of scarcity. And yet the Bible repeatedly tells stories of abundance because the logic and appeal of scarcity does not disappear with the arrival of abundance. Even when God graciously provides all that is needed in the wilderness, for example, people still find themselves hungry for something more, something else, or something different. Though the issues are enormously complex, and I do not imagine that we will find clear resolution of the food issues in a probe of biblical texts, a focus on hunger may permit us to think afresh and faithfully on these urgent questions. Why hunger?

- Because everyone has to eat; "bread" is our most elemental requirement;
- because food *production* raises environmental issues, for a diminished environment will not and cannot "bring forth" as intended;
- because food *consumption* leads to a cluster of issues around "consumerism" and the mad pursuit of more commodities, in the futile hope that they will make us safe and happy;
- because food *distribution* raises economic questions between haves and have-nots, about who gets what, on what terms, and by whose decision;

3

- because there is an overlap between "hunger for food" and "spiritual hunger," and the connection and tension between the two is crucial for our common life.[1]

In short "hunger" touches the great practical questions of our contemporary world and drives us back to theological wonderment.

I

Given the theme of "hunger," I suggest that we understand our situation as a "food fight." The struggle for food between those who have advantage, resources, markets, and leverage and those who lack those advantages is a long-term fight that is waged in many modes. Given these many modes, however, the great struggles are finally about "bread," with the term "bread" standing for all the dimensions of wealth, control, status, and the capacity to be an agent in one's own history.

The Bible itself is a venue for that long-term food fight, that is, a struggle between competing ways to think about food and hunger. The fight for food is a fight between ideologies about food, or theologies about food, or explanatory narratives about food. That tension in the Bible itself is a counterpoint to the tension we ourselves know about. Each of us is variously involved in a food fight concerning the legitimacy of our own hungers and the pressure of the hungers of others that impinge upon our cache of food. In the midst of that struggle, which is grandly biblical and acutely personal, we carry on an inquiry about what is right and what is true, what is permitted and what is required.

In these first two chapters I will trace these two ideologies (theologies, explanatory narratives) of food to consider how that food fight may matter to local congregations. By connecting a sequence of texts, I want to show that there is continuity and a coherent logic to each of these ideologies, and that they are in profound tension with each other.

Here is my thesis for the first of these trajectories that I will line out: One stance in the food fight is a system of food production, distribution, and consumption that is based on the conviction that the world is a closed system of limited resources. The accent is upon scarcity. The emotive result is anxiety about not having enough. The practical consequences consist in practices and policies of accumulation that aim at monopoly.

The purpose of a monopoly of food resources and supplies is the offer of a "final solution" to the food crisis. The defining terms of this ideology, then, are *scarcity*, *anxiety*, *accumulation*, and *monopoly*. The enactment of this ideology consists in consumerism (which in health may lead to obesity and in policy may lead to agribusiness that seeks to compel all the production possible), protected by a strong military that secures and guarantees the perpetuation of the entire system.

## II

In the Old Testament Pharaoh is the agent, symbol, and metaphor for a food system that is rooted in anxious scarcity and enacted in accumulation on the way to monopoly. It is plausible that Pharaoh in the book of Exodus is a nameable (but unnamed) historical figure; scholarship has used great energy trying to identify him. But beyond whatever he may have been historically, Pharaoh functions as the recurring agent of anxious scarcity, which makes the exodus narrative endlessly contemporary and always transferable to a new context. Pharaoh's endless mantra is "Make more bricks" (Exod. 5:4–19). The bricks are in order to construct more storehouse cities (Exod. 1:11). And the function of the storehouse cities is to accumulate more food, more grain, until Pharaoh controls all of it. He is presented in the narrative as one who wants, with an insatiable appetite for more! A series of texts tell the story of this great accumulator:

1. At the very beginning of the Israelite story in Genesis 12, in the second paragraph concerning Abraham and Sarah, Pharaoh already appears. Indeed, Israel cannot tell its story of covenantal alternative without reference to Pharaoh, who is the indispensable durable counterpoint. In Genesis 12:10, it is reported that a famine caused Abraham to go to Egypt for food. The matter is not explained. It is an assumption of the narrative that when everyone else is out of food, Pharaoh still will have food. Pharaoh of course has food because the

Nile River is endlessly productive, and because Pharaoh is a genius at administrative authority and knows how to work the irrigation system and make the trains run on time. But beyond that, he is a monopolizer who has the capacity to defy even a circumstance of famine.

The narrative is terse but nevertheless reports that Pharaoh was attracted to Sarah, beautiful wife of Abraham, and "the woman was taken into Pharaoh's house" (12:15). From the outset women have been a bargaining chip in the food fight among powerful men. The fact that the narrative resolves the treatment of Sarah does not detract from the plot line concerning the avarice of Pharaoh, who assumed, given his food monopoly, that he was entitled to whatever he could possess.

2. A long time later in the narrative, in Genesis 41, it is reported that Pharaoh had two nightmares. The first dream concerns seven sleek and fat cows that were devoured by seven cows that were thin and ugly (41:1–4). The second bad dream concerned seven ears of grain that were plump and good. And seven ears of grain that were thin and blighted swallowed up the seven good ears (vv. 5–7). Like every dream, these dreams are vivid and concrete, and we are to notice the contrast:

> *Cows*: sleek and fat / ugly and thin;
> *Ears of grain*: plump and full / thin and blighted.

The contrast bespeaks indulgent well-being and parsimonious stress. In the nightmares, moreover, the thin stuff prevails and defeats the good stuff. The verbs, "ate, swallowed," are verbs of food ingestion. So these are food dreams.

Pharaoh was troubled in the morning. He could vividly remember the dreams; but he did not understand them. He consulted with his intelligence community, perhaps even the credentialed therapist of his realm. None could tell him the meaning, though none doubted that the dreams had a meaning. It is remarkable, moreover, that the narrator knows the dream. How could an Israelite narrator know the dreams of Pharaoh? Well, because covenantal folk know about the nightmares that accumulators invariably have. They know that accumulators live, always, on orange alert. The narrator notices, but does not underscore, the irony that the one with the most is the one who has the most acute dreams of loss.

3. Pharaoh had to reach outside his entourage in order to get an interpretation of the dreams. Perhaps all of his advisors were so narcotized by the monopoly in which they lived that none could penetrate the hidden messages of the dreams that witnessed against the monopoly. It is like asking the chair of a great bureaucracy to pause over a poem that is likely to be misread as a memo. But Pharaoh finds an interpreter. He finds Joseph, a young Hebrew who was a jailed outsider, regarded as an enemy of the state. He is cleaned up, shaven, given proper clothes, and brought before Pharaoh, the accumulator (41:14). Pharaoh patiently tells Joseph his dreams, using the terms of contrast, "fat and sleek, poor, ugly, and thin," "full and good, withered, thin, and blighted." The terms are repeated, but with two additions. Now the cows are "poor" and the stalks of grain are "withered." In the retelling, the extremities of the bad in the dreams are underlined.

Joseph knows immediately, because, says he, it is "not I" but God who will interpret. The dreams are about the coming famine that will be "very grievous" (v. 31). The irony is that the one with everything has a nightmare about loss. The peasants who had little likely had no such dream, because they had not enough to lose.

4. The nightmare, now interpreted, is grounded in anxiety and leads to new policy. Anxiety drives policy! Imagine a great superpower that is anxious about loss in a way that leads to new policy! Pharaoh seeks an administrator to manage the nightmare crisis that is coming. Joseph recommends that Pharaoh find someone who is "discerning and wise" (v. 33). Unsurprisingly, Joseph himself is the only candidate for the post. Before he is nominated, Joseph presents a plan to Pharaoh about how to manage the scarcity to come. It is like the worst-case scenario of planning procedure in the war office. Pharaoh is taken with the plan and appoints Joseph:

> You shall be over my house, and all my people shall order themselves as you command; only with regard to the throne will I be greater than you. (Gen. 41:40)

The narrator pauses, even in the midst of the crisis, to celebrate the appointment (see vv. 42–45). It is a big deal that this Israelite will take care of the nightmare of food scarcity that has already propelled the great accumulator toward monopoly.

5. The move from nightmare to policy is reported in Genesis 47:13–26, wherein Joseph introduces draconian food policies. The peasants, without food of their own, had successively to bargain away their money, then their livestock, then their land, and finally their bodies. In exchange for food from the great accumulator, they became Pharaoh's slaves. That is how we reach the slave narrative of the book of Exodus. Slavery as a given in the book of Exodus is the outcome of the food policies of monopoly in the book of Genesis. The force of monopoly is so acute that by the end of the narrative, the newly recruited slaves, victims of the food policy of Pharaoh, are grateful for their own enslavement. They say, "You have saved our lives; may it please my lord, we will be slaves to Pharaoh" (v. 25). The ideology of Pharaoh is now all-encompassing. Even the slaves echo it back to the big house. And the narrator adds laconically:

> So Joseph bought all the land of Egypt for Pharaoh. . . . The land of the priests alone did not become Pharaoh's. (vv. 20, 26)

The narrator does not call attention to the irony that the implementation of the food policy of monopoly that eventuated in slavery is accomplished by an Israelite! Leon Kass characterizes the narrative achievement as the full "Egyptianization" of Joseph.[2] Pharaoh's ideology of monopoly is so totalizing that none could resist it, not even an Israelite who might have known better. Everything yields to the force of monopoly!

Thus Pharaoh in his massive power, supported by an ideology of supreme authority, could imagine himself autonomous and free to do what he wanted. He lived in great arrogance, not imagining that his power to control had any limit. In the belated criticism of Pharaoh in the Bible, the limit on monopolizing power is voiced in poetic prophetic utterances. For example, Isaiah can imagine that the Nile that made Pharaoh's breadbasket is at the behest of YHWH, the Creator, who will curb Pharaoh's self-indulgence by drying it up (see Isa. 19:5–7). But of course such prophetic imagination lies well beyond Pharaoh . . . or Joseph. They are practical men who move from their nightmare of scarcity, and by their immense social force they imagine they can fend off the threats about which they dream in their haunted nights.

## III

It is easy enough to establish Pharaoh as the "bad guy" in the Israelite narrative. He was an easy target that evoked no sympathy in Israel. But remarkably, Pharaoh's ideology of scarcity, anxiety, accumulation, and monopoly could not be kept at pharaonic distance. It entered right into the midst of Israel's own life in a way that skewed and distorted Israel's covenantal faith.

1. As the tradition stands, they could see it coming. They could anticipate the force of this ideology in their own midst. It may be that such foreboding is "after the fact," when they saw the impact of that ideology on their common life. But even if it is a retrospect, it is presented as a foreboding. In Deuteronomy 17:14–20, the only Torah commandment on kingship, Moses warns against the power of accumulation, because accumulation aimed at monopoly contradicts covenant:

> [Your coming king] must not acquire many horses for himself, or return the people to Egypt in order to acquire more horses . . . And he must not acquire many wives for himself, or else his heart will turn away; also silver and gold he must not acquire in great quantity for himself. (vv. 16–17)

The recurring favorites of all accumulators are "horses, women, silver, and gold." But all of that is only "food" writ large, an effort at self-securing, never to lack.

The alert of the Torah is matched by Samuel's speech anticipating the coming of monarchy in Israel:

> These will be the ways of the king who will reign over you: he will take your sons and appoint them to his chariots and to be his horsemen, and to run before his chariots . . . and some to plow his ground and to reap his harvest, and to make his implements of war and the equipment of his chariots. He will take your daughters to be perfumers and cooks and bakers. He will take the best of your fields and vineyards and olive orchards and give them to his courtiers. He will take one-tenth of your grain and of your vineyards and give it to his officers and his courtiers. He will take your male and female slaves, and the best of your cattle and donkeys, and put them to his work. He will take one-tenth of your flocks, and you shall be his slaves. (1 Sam. 8:11–17)

The operative word is "take." The subject is taxation and the draft. But the undercurrent is that the king will have an insatiable appetite. The accumulator will seize your grain and flocks (food) and reduce all to slavery. The horrified anticipation is that organized greed will skew all social relationships in the interest of aggrandizement, and the confiscation will run from food to the military, an undifferentiated package in a world of organized appetites.

2. In retrospect, these anticipations in Deuteronomy 17 and 1 Samuel 8 were in fact responses to the regime of Solomon, who radically shifted the society of Israel away from a covenantal economy to an economy of accumulation, in which the strong could take from the weak in the service of an uncurbed appetite for more. In the horizon of Israel, Solomon becomes the great embodiment of *scarcity*, *anxiety*, *accumulation*, and *monopoly*. Who would have thought that Israel's covenantal commitments were so readily vulnerable to the incursion of Pharaoh's ideology? Well, Solomon even becomes Pharaoh's son-in-law (1 Kgs. 3:1; 7:8; 9:24; 11:1). It takes no imagination to think that Solomon set out to prove to his in-laws that he was competent in their great game of greedy self-indulgence. And so Solomon is portrayed in 1 Kings 3–11 as the full practitioner of the ideology of accumulation:

First Kings 4:1–6 reports on the king's bureaucracy, an organization of power that some interpreters believe was appropriated from Egyptian models. The last named official, Adoniram son of Abda, was secretary of labor, but here it is "forced labor," coerced labor in the service of the crown. The term, recurring in Solomonic reports, echoes Pharaoh's labor policy. The regime has reduced free members of society into service to the crown, most especially for the construction of self-aggrandizing monuments to monopoly: the temple (1 Kgs. 5:13–18), his fortifications, his palaces, and his storehouses (9:15–23). That latter report ends: "These were the chief officers who were over Solomon's work; five hundred and fifty, who had charge of the people who carried on the work" (9:23). It must have been a huge workforce to require 550 supervisors, a vast program that claimed the resources and people-power of society, all in the service of royal anxiety.

The project costs lots of money. Thus in 1 Kings 4:7–19 we have an organizational chart finely detailing Solomon's tax-collecting apparatus. It is clear that there were no exemptions from taxation that transferred wealth from peasants to urban elites. Moreover, two of the tax officials, Ben-abinadad (v. 11) and Ahimaaz (v. 15), were Solomon's sons-in-law. Thus the report suggests a close network of urban elites who were committed to a common process of accumulation.

3. The payout of forced labor (4:6) and tax arrangements (vv. 7–19) is the report concerning the royal appetite for food:

> Solomon's provision for one day was thirty cors of choice flour, and sixty cors of meal, ten fat oxen, and twenty pasture-fed cattle, one hundred sheep, besides deer, gazelles, roebucks, and fatted fowl. (vv. 22–23)

It is remarkable that in the midst of all the grand royal schemes, the narrative pauses over food. The appetite of the regime is broad and deep. The economic base for such provision was not only taxes and cheap labor but also tribute from foreign lands (protection money) and tariff revenue, all in the interest of accumulation. The outcome is an ostentatious self-exhibit that came to mark every part of the urban confiscation that depended on the produce of the disempowered peasants.

The extravagance of food is a kind of symbol in the script of Solomon for systemic accumulation on every front. Thus:

- The exhibition of wealth is replicated in the temple that overflows with extravagant gold (1 Kgs. 6:19–22; 7:48–51).
- The accumulation of songs and proverbs posit Solomon as a patron of the arts with a monopoly on beauty and wisdom (4:29–34).
- The trade in arms (horses and chariots) suggests that he had a monopoly on the flow of arms due to his strategic geographic location (10:26–29).
- He enjoyed lavish tribute from foreign powers, all offered in deference and submissiveness, to his international enhancement (10:14–25).
- Eventually he is condemned for his accumulation of women (700 princesses and 300 concubines), women being one more accoutrement to an over-the-top extravagance, perhaps trophy wives for exhibit.

On exhibit is this imagined superpower in its capacity to turn everything and everyone into a collectible commodity, in order to capture the imagination of Israel and of the other powers as well, notably the Queen of Sheba (10:1–10). This presentation of Solomon, I believe, does not witness to personal greed. Rather, it attests the power of the ideology of accumulation that entranced Israel. In such an arrangement, inevitably the hunger of the peasants, the real food hunger of the disadvantaged, disappears from the screen of policy and practice. Outside of this ideological venue, there is no one left to notice. The logic of accumulation is secure:

- If there is scarcity, get all you can.
- If there is not enough, do not share.
- If others want some, they are a threat to be repelled.

## IV

The deep critique of the ideology of accumulation is voiced by the prophetic tradition that sounds with immense emotive force and rigorous theological authority. The prophetic tradition repeatedly takes aim precisely at the ideology of scarcity and anxiety that produced accumulation aimed at monopoly.

1. A somewhat soft form of critique is the narrative of Elisha, who proceeded to solve the food problem of ancient Israel without engagement with or even acknowledgment of the ideology of accumulation.

- In the narrative of 2 Kings 4:1–7, Elisha provides the widow mother with enough oil to pay her creditors and save her son. She is, moreover, dependent upon her village neighbors to help her catch the oil that will save her life and the life of her son. We should not miss the framing of the narrative as an instance of the food fight between creditors and debtors. The creditors—surely the urban elites—are about to enslave her son for her debt, a practice as old as Pharaoh and as recent as Solomon. Elisha, without pedigree or credential, enacts abundance that defies the ideology of scarcity and negates the credit system of the accumulators. Perhaps the most "miraculous" aspect here is in fact the common mystery of "abundance" that is accepted among the peasants.

- In 2 Kings 4:42–44, Elisha again participates in the ongoing food fight by feeding a hundred people with some food left over. The narrative is terse and without explanation. Elisha clearly performs in a way that is outside of and in contradiction to the accumulation system.

2. When we move from narrative to poetry, the critique of the accumulation system is much more prevalent and poignant. I will begin with two texts from Amos.

- In Amos 6:4–7, Amos pronounces a "woe" on those who are "at ease in Zion."[3] He begins with an inventory of self-indulgences among those who have too much time on their hands:

> Alas for those who lie on beds of ivory,
>     and lounge on their couches,
> and eat lambs from the flock,
>     and calves from the stall;
> who sing idle songs to the sound of the harp,
>     and like David improvise on instruments of music;
> who drink wine from bowls,
>     and anoint themselves with the finest oils.
>                                                    Amos 6:4–6

The poem turns on the conjunction "but" in verse 6:

> *but* are not grieved over the ruin of Joseph.

The critique is not of their self-indulgence, but of the resultant indifference to social reality. The social crisis that Amos sees (that they do not see) is that "Joseph" (i.e., Israel) is a failed community. As every prophetic poet knows, the practitioners of self-indulgence at the expense of others are characteristically the last to notice that what they regard as a blessing is in fact a deep pathology that will in the end destroy what they most value. The self-indulgent are so dulled and incapable of social awareness or social criticism that they do not reckon with reality.

The payout of the oracle is the "therefore" of verse 7:

> *Therefore* they shall now be the first to go into exile,
>     and the revelry of the loungers shall pass away.

The ones most secure will be the most threatened. And the accumulation of excessive goods will offer no protection from the incursions of history that sound here as divine judgment.

• In 8:4–8 Amos addresses those whose wealth is linked to dishonest exploitation of the poor. He does not here mention tax or credit arrangements, only the use of dishonest weights in commerce. But the outcome, says he, is the same. The land will "tremble," likely at the pounding of the invading Assyrian army. It is not incidental that the poetic unit ends with reference to the rise and fall of the Nile River. While the reference is to the reliability of the river, the evocation of Egypt is a reminder in Israel that nobody, not even the land of Egypt, escapes the reality of God's governance. This God is not finally mocked by the monopoly of the market as wealth is transferred from the poor and needy by commercial means.

3. Isaiah 3 offers a long poem about the opposition of YHWH to a culture of accumulation. As in 1 Samuel 8, the governing verb is "take away" (Isa. 3:1, 18). The poem anticipates the loss in Jerusalem of all the commodity finery so valued in the city. In the poetry, the God of covenant stands in opposition to commodity accumulation. To accent the point, the prophet delights to detail the accumulation of goods that will be lost:

> In that day the Lord will take away the finery of the anklets, the headbands, and the crescents; the pendants, the bracelets, and the scarfs; the headdresses, the armlets, the sashes, the perfume boxes, and the amulets; the signet rings and nose rings; the festal robes, the mantles, the cloaks, and the handbags; the garments of gauze, the linen garments, the turbans, and the veils. (vv. 18–23)

The inventory alludes to exhibitionism in Jerusalem:

> Because the daughters of Zion are haughty
>   and walk with outstretched necks,
>     glancing wantonly with their eyes,
>   mincing along as they go,
>     tinkling with their feet.
>
>                               Isa. 3:16

All of that will be lost, because the God of covenant will undo the accumulation system. The prophet knows, as does the foundational covenantal tradition, that such commodity accumulation depends finally upon social exploitation. The indictment concerns abuse of the vulnerable poor:

> It is you who have devoured the vineyard;
> the spoil of the poor is in your houses.
> What do you mean by crushing my people,
> by grinding the face of the poor? says the Lord GOD of hosts.
>
> Isa. 3:14b–15

The "poor" constitute that segment of the population that is turned, through exploitation, into dispensable commodity. But it cannot stand! That food system, says the poet, has no future.

4. Finally I mention a remarkable text in Ezekiel. In his emotive critique of Jerusalem in its self-indulgent infidelity, Ezekiel likens the Holy City (and its self-indulgent population) to ancient, remembered Sodom. He contrasts Jerusalem to Sodom:

> Your sister Sodom and her daughters have not done as you and your daughters have done. (Ezek. 16:48)

The affront of Sodom, says he, was self-indulgence:

> This was the guilt of your sister Sodom: she and her daughters had pride, excess of food, and prosperous ease, but did not aid the poor and needy. They were haughty, and did abominable things before me. (vv. 49–50)

For that, Sodom was destroyed; and Jerusalem is worse! In the horizon of Ezekiel, the defining sin of Sodom, and by inference of Jerusalem, is pride expressed as excess of food that precluded care of the poor and needy. The argument is the same as elsewhere. Arrogant autonomy, expressed as excessive consumption, generated indifference to the poor and needy. Such indifference, which makes perfect sense in the ideology of accumulation, is unbearable in the world that YHWH governs. The oracle ends with severity:

> You must bear the penalty of your lewdness and your abominations. (v. 58)

It is impossible to appreciate the cumulative effect of prophetic poetry unless we see that it joins issue with an ideology that is, in their judgment, in deep contradiction to the true character of Israel and certainly to the true intent of YHWH, who presides over Israel and the food supply.

## V

The monopolizers keep supplying the prophets with a multitude of case studies. At the beginning there is Pharaoh, who needs more bricks. In Jerusalem there is Solomon, who eats too well. Then, at the other end of the Old Testament, is Nebuchadnezzar, the great king of Babylon, who destroyed Jerusalem. Like Pharaoh, Nebuchadnezzar became a metaphor and a cipher for all monopolizers, yet another embodiment of the food fight.

1. Jeremiah anticipates his coming army, even though, in the poetry, he does not specifically name him. The poet imagines the coming of the army of Nebuchadnezzar that will be strong, strange, huge, and powerful, sweeping all before it. The great devourer is sent by YHWH against YHWH's own city (see Jer. 5:15–16). And then the poet describes what this army, like every invading army, will do to the land:

> They shall eat up your harvest and your food;
>     they shall eat up your sons and your daughters;
> they shall eat up your flocks and your herds;
>     they shall eat up your vines and your fig trees.
>                                                      Jer. 5:17

The poem uses the word "eat" four times. Talk about a food fight! The great superpower will confiscate all the food sources of the vulnerable city,

- from harvest to food,
- from sons to daughters,
- from flocks to herds,
- from vines to fig trees.

That is what superpowers do, in their appetite for control, to vulnerable subject states.

2. No wonder Isaiah chides Babylon for acting as if it were autonomous:

You said, "I shall be mistress forever." . . .
[You] say in your heart,
"I am, and there is no one besides me." . . .
[Y]ou said, "No one sees me." . . .
"I am, and there is no one besides me."
Isa. 47:7, 8, 10

When a superpower imagines that it is autonomous and not account-able, then it can eat all the food, take all the resources, gobble up all the treasures, exhaust all the reserves, and never answer. It belongs to the strong in the food fight, says Jeremiah, to "have no mercy" (Jer. 6:23). When food is managed without mercy, abuse, suffering, and slavery are sure to eventuate.

3. I cite one other Babylonian text that is a little quirky but per-haps illuminating. Now the king is Belshazzar, son of Nebuchadnez-zar; he is a stand-in for his father, who is a stand-in for Antiochus IV Epiphanes, who is a stand-in for all monopolizers. The narrator reports:

King Belshazzar made a great festival for a thousand of his lords, and he was drinking wine in the presence of the thousand. (Dan. 5:1)

Of course, that is what the strong in the food fight do. They give feasts. They invite all the powerful, in order to exhibit their success. The din-ner is ostentatious, not unlike lavish government dinners, and then:

Belshazzar commanded that they bring in the vessels of gold and silver that his father Nebuchadnezzar had taken out of the temple in Jerusalem. (v. 2)

The point of lavish enjoyment from the temple vessels is to scandal-ize the Jews who watched their holy vessels used for such fluff. The narrative teems with self-indulgence and mocks the pretense. And then in verse 5, finally, it is reported:

Immediately the fingers of a human hand appeared and began writing on the plaster of the wall of the royal palace, next to the lampstand.

The words are in code, and none of the intelligence community of the sated empire can decode them. But the appearance of the writing itself terrifies the king (Dan. 5:6–7, 9). The queen tries to ease the king's anxiety by summoning Daniel, the Jew, who knew the codes of hidden wisdom. Daniel refuses royal rewards; but he reads the wall to the king:

> You have exalted yourself against the Lord of heaven! The vessels of his temple have been brought in before you, and you and your lords, your wives and your concubines have been drinking wine from them. You have praised the gods of silver and gold, of bronze, iron, wood, and stone, which do not see or hear or know; but the God in whose power is your very breath, and to whom belong all your ways, you have not honored. (v. 23)

It follows, on the wall, that the kingdom will end. The narrative concludes tersely, "That very night Belshazzar, the Chaldean king, was killed" (v. 30). The banquet is interrupted. Those who indulge at the expense of the peasants cannot eat in peace. Such indulgence is short-term, because alongside the peasants there is the great God, who eventually will not be mocked. Belshazzar must, yet again, learn the lesson of his greedy father, Nebuchadnezzar (see vv. 20–21). The lesson is repeatedly offered to the perpetrators of the food fight. Those monopolizers regularly learn too late.

# VI

Eventually our study of food comes to Jesus, who clearly violated the rules of the food system by eating with publicans and sinners (Mark 2:16).[4] And the rules of eating are, of course, the rules of power. Thus when policy-makers opine that businesses are private and should serve whom they want, it is understood as an endorsement of a power arrangement that seeks to be beyond challenge. Jesus violates the rules and thereby presents himself as an enemy of those rules and those power arrangements. I cite three texts from Luke.

1. It is no wonder that in the Magnificat, the song of Mary that is the theme song of Luke, Mary sang of food:

> He has filled the hungry with good things,
>     and sent the rich away empty.
> Luke 1:53

Mary anticipates that the narrative to follow in Luke will be witness to a food revolution whereby the old rules of food are overthrown so that all may share.

2. In Luke 14, Jesus teaches his host at dinner:

> When you give a luncheon or a dinner, do not invite your friends or your brothers or your relatives or rich neighbors, in case they may invite you in return, and you would be repaid. But when you give a banquet, invite the poor, the crippled, the lame, and the blind. And you will be blessed, because they cannot repay you, for you will be repaid at the resurrection of the righteous. (Luke 14:12–14)

Jesus redefines the social process of eating in an inclusive way. And then he tells his parable of the great banquet. When the honored guests are too busy to attend, the master of the table wants the household filled with those who are on the "streets and lanes" (v. 21), that is, the street people not usually qualified for such a bountiful table.

3. In Luke 12, Jesus tells a parable about a rich man who prospered in agriculture. He frames the story as a warning about greed. And then we watch as the prosperous man wants to store more and more. But his food production is so abundant that he finally can say:

> "What should I do, for I have no place to store my crops?" Then he said, "I will do this: I will pull down my barns and build larger ones, and there I will store all my grain and my goods." (Luke 12:17–18)

And then he said to himself:

> Soul, you have ample goods laid up for many years; relax, eat, drink, and be merry. (v. 19)

This is a guy who has made it in the food world. He builds bigger barns, bigger silos, bigger granaries, and bigger vaults. In wanting more storehouses for his monopoly of food, he sounds like Pharaoh, who built storage cities, as did Solomon (1 Kgs. 9:19). They are all of a piece, those who secured a disproportionate share of the world's food supply.

And then in the parable, "But God said to him" (Luke 12:20). The interruption of such self-congratulations sounds like the word of

YHWH to Pharaoh, "Let my people go." It reads like the handwriting on the wall to Belshazzar. And like that story, this story ends with the guy dead that night. Food monopolizers are all, sooner or later, interrupted by this inscrutable master of all food.

And then Jesus turns the parable of Luke 12 into an instruction for his disciples in the next verse:

> Therefore I tell you, do not worry about your life, what you will eat, or about your body, what you will wear. (Luke 12:22)

Do not participate in the anxiety system that is grounded in a mistaken notion of scarcity. Do not be anxious, because your heavenly Father, the Food Manager, knows what you need. Then Jesus observes birds and lilies that are not anxious, because they trust the Creator who gives them their food supply. After birds and lilies, we get this familiar zinger that is so familiar that we may not notice that it is a zinger:

> Yet I tell you, even Solomon in all his glory was not clothed like one of these. (v. 27)

Not even Solomon! Not even the great accumulator! Not even Pharaoh! Not even Nebuchadnezzar! Not even Belshazzar! Not any of the accumulators can get outside the anxiety that is intrinsic to the scarcity system.

So, to review, the crisis of scarcity, anxiety, accumulation, and monopoly:

- touches *food consumption* and asks about commoditization;
- touches *food distribution* and the redistribution of food at the Creator's behest;
- touches the environment that overproduces in order to add to the monopoly.

It makes one wonder if the monopolizers had any capacity for an internal life, what they did about their hunger for meaning, whether they noticed the neighbor when they gathered at the table. It keeps ringing in our ears: "Not even Solomon in all his glory" . . . in all his self-indulgence.

The biblical text traces the career of the monopolizers. But it does more than that. It attests that there is another way to do food. When our granaries and our bodies store surpluses, our bodies and the body politic suffer. It can be otherwise: We can meet at the table in another way. We watch and notice while it is taken, blessed, broken, and given. And there is always more than enough, sometimes twelve baskets, sometimes seven baskets; it is shared and ample. No need to accumulate!

## Questions for Reflection

1. Where do you see anxiety about scarcity in society today, particularly around food production, consumption, and distribution? In what other areas of current culture do you see people and policies affected by the crisis of scarcity, anxiety, accumulation, and monopoly?

2. In reflecting on Pharaoh's dreams, Brueggemann points out "the irony that the one with the most is the one who has the most acute dreams of loss" (p. 6). Can you think of other examples of accumulation leading to anxiety about loss that then spurred unhealthy practices and attitudes? How do you understand Joseph's role in Pharaoh's anxiety and the resulting food policies that lead to the impoverishment and enslavement of Israel?

3. We read about the "power of the ideology of accumulation that entranced Israel" and Solomon, turning "everything and everyone into a collectible commodity" (p. 12). How is that power at work today? What current prophets and poets do you know of who are speaking about these issues?

4. What other stories about Jesus can you think of that demonstrate his revolutionary way of approaching food and the power structures entangled with it?

Chapter 2

# Food Fight II

## Abundance, Trust, Gratitude, and Sharing

### Community: Abundant Food Practice as Astonished Gratitude

There is amazing news for those who trust too much in the ideology of *scarcity, anxiety, accumulation,* and *monopoly.* There is an alternative to that ideology that leads to a different daily life in faith and practice. This alternative way invites a move:

- from scarcity to *abundance*
- from anxiety to *trust*
- from accumulation to *sharing*
- from monopoly to *covenantal neighborliness*

My topic in this second chapter is this "other way" of obedient trust that leads to sharing and culminates in covenantal neighborliness. This other theological conviction runs through the Bible, but not easily or uninterruptedly, because the ideology of scarcity and anxiety also occupies a lot of the text. Thus the Bible itself exhibits the food fight and is congruent with the way the food fight exists among us, and indeed exists, for each of us, in our own persons.

In the first chapter I exposited the theology of scarcity and anxiety as it pertains to food and hunger. In this chapter I consider the alternative that is exhibited in God's generosity that evokes the gratitude of Israel and the church. That alternative permits us, on a daily basis, to be astonished by divine generosity that yields gratitude rather than anxiety.

I

The "other way" in the food fight is grounded in creation faith, in the conviction that the world is God's creation that is designed to exhibit and enact God's good will for abundant life. The great creation text in Genesis 1 that opens the Bible is not about "origins." It is about the claim that the world is deeply linked to God's will and purpose. The world for that reason is not a closed system that operates on its own, leaving us with a zero-sum game; it is rather a process open to the continued gifts of the Creator. Yet the world does not possess the gift of life on its own. Creation is God's partner, God's object, God's vehicle for wellness in the world that God continues to enact in the ongoing work of creation.[1] The Genesis recital tells of the ordered goodness of the world that moves progressively from day to day until it arrives at "very good" (Gen. 1:31). That ordered goodness, moreover, is sustained and reliable, even in the face of the deep threat of chaos. Thus, at the conclusion of the flood narrative, after the power of chaos has done its worst, God declares:

> As long as the earth endures,
>     seedtime and harvest, cold and heat,
> summer and winter, day and night,
>     shall not cease.
>
> Gen. 8:22

The full, regular functioning of the creation is assured by divine decree!

The recital has two features that concern us. First, the world is blessed by God. God had committed God's own life-giving force into the wonder of the world. Second, the effect of that divine blessing bestowed on the world is that the world is to be fruitful, to keep generating food that will sustain all of life:

> God blessed them, saying, "Be fruitful and multiply and fill the waters in the seas, and let birds multiply on the earth." (Gen. 1:22)

That life-giving force, moreover, has been entrusted to human care and supervision:

"See, I have *given you* every plant yielding seed that is upon the face of all the earth, . . . and you shall have them for food. And to every beast of the earth, and to every bird of the air, and to everything that creeps on the earth, everything that has the breath of life, I have given every *green* plant for food." And it was so. (Gen. 1:29–30, italics added)

Right from the start, the Creator has known that *green* is the color of earthly well-being!

The relationship of creator and creatureliness is one of committed trust and responding obedience. The news is that the world is articulated in personal-interpersonal categories, that the proper interaction of God and world, creator and creature, is one of dialogic interaction that features trust, generosity, gratitude, and obedience. Such a way in the world refuses the flat, reductionist language of commodity and control to which market ideology is always tempted. Thus the Bible can imagine that all creatures—humans as well as birds, beasts, and fish—are in conversation with the Creator.

Specifically that conversation, as concerns human persons, is in the form of prayer. The most pertinent prayer for the food fight is the simple, regular table prayer that voices thanks to God for food and that acknowledges that food is a gift from God and not a human product or possession. That prayer, practiced on every occasion of receiving food, is one of gratitude that contradicts the self-sufficiency of the accumulators. In the Old Testament, the two most treasured table prayers are situated in psalms of creation. In Psalm 145, the psalm acknowledges God's "wondrous works" of generosity that outrun human expectation (vv. 4–7). The psalm identifies, in stylized terms, the covenantal fidelity of God as "gracious and merciful" (vv. 8–9) and invites all creatures to give thanks:

> All your works shall give thanks to you, O LORD,
>     and all your faithful shall bless you.
> Ps. 145:10

Then, in verses 15–16, comes what has long been a reiterated table prayer:

> The eyes of all look to you,
>     and you give them their food in due season.

> You open your hand,
>     satisfying the desire of every living thing.

The prayer affirms that God feeds "every living creature"; there is a correlation between "desire" and the timely generosity of God the Creator, who responds to every hunger. The prayer is a defiant refusal of autonomy and self-sufficiency.

The second such prayer is in Psalm 104, a psalm that moves from the large framing of creation as "heaven, earth, and the waters" (vv. 2–9) to the specificities of daily life:

> You cause the grass to grow for the cattle,
>     and plants for people to use,
> to bring forth food from the earth,
>     and wine to gladden the human heart,
> oil to make the face shine,
>     and bread to strengthen the human heart.
> Ps. 104:14–15

We may notice two things about this list of daily provisions of wine, oil, and bread. The three derive from grapes (wine), olives (oil), and grain (bread). These are the three great money crops in the ancient world, "grain, wine, and oil" (Deut. 7:13; 14:23; Neh. 13:5; Isa. 36:17; Hos. 2:8; Joel 2:19). But these cash crops that are raised by peasants (and often exploited by the accumulators) are also the sacramental tokens of the church: thus water for baptism, bread and wine for the Eucharist, and oil for anointing. These sacramental claims of the church take the core stuff of creation's fullness as signs of the goodness and presence of God in the world.

While God is celebrated in large scope and then in regular provision, the psalm comes down to the case of daily food:

> These all look to you
>     to give them their food in due season;
> when you give it to them, they gather it up;
>     when you open your hand, they are filled with good things.
> Ps. 104:27–28

It is God's open hand that feeds "all" who finally rely upon the Creator. The creaturely look to the generous Creator is one of astonishment, awe, wonder, and gratitude, that the Genesis Creator would mobilize such a food-producing energy for such vulnerable cases as carrots, whales, possums, and "us." The prayer affirms, "These all look to you," an expectant, trustful look; the language is paralleled in Psalm 145:15, "The eyes of all look to you." The grateful look is one of glad dependence that God will provide.

Such was the "look of Adam" toward the Creator. That was *the look* in the first instance of being formed. But that look is also present in awed gratitude every time there is food. It is the gift of food from the Creator that valorizes the creature. Such a look is a look of wonder for food given generously, a verification that our life—all of life—is sustained in well-being and joy. That look is such an antithesis to the blank stare of the accumulator, who has only a look of self-congratulations. That look of Adam is one of yielding trust and gratitude. Food is sustenance, valorization, and the meeting of elemental desire.

## II

The "other way"—other than accumulation—is rooted in the conviction that the Creator God presides over an abundant food supply with generosity toward all creatures. This conviction cannot be stated with scientific precision or with closely reasoned logic, and Israel never tried to do so. The reality of divine abundance given in generosity requires a very different mode of discourse, namely, doxology. Doxology is the glad, self-abandoning exuberance of the creature who holds nothing back in affirmation of the Creator.[2] Doxology is a mode of discourse that matches the lived generosity of the creation. Indeed, Genesis 1 itself has the cadences of doxology, the lining out of awe that cannot be articulated in scientific discourse. The psalms that I have cited are full, extended doxologies that take in the scope of all creation. Psalm 104 celebrates the framing of creation (vv. 1–9) but pivots on *the gift of water*, and this in an arid climate:

> You make springs gush forth in the valleys;
>     they flow between the hills,
> giving drink to every wild animal;
>     the wild asses quench their thirst.
> By the streams the birds of the air have their habitation;

> they sing among the branches.
> From your lofty abode you water the mountains;
>     the earth is satisfied with the fruit of your work.
>                                               Ps. 104:10–13

The water here is the same water that flows in the four rivers of the garden of Eden (Gen. 2:10–14); it is clear that water is what makes a life-giving world possible. The psalm notices the sustenance of all creatures from the water-providing God—wild animals, wild asses, birds, cattle, storks, wild goats, coneys, lions. It is no wonder that at verse 24 the psalmist must fall back in exuberance, lacking any other form of adequate speech (see also v. 35):

> O LORD, how manifold are your works!
>     In wisdom you have made them all;
>     the earth is full of your creatures.

The secret of creation is pronounced in verses 29–30 by the double reference to God's "spirit/breath" on which the world depends. The world is not a self-starter. It cannot maintain itself automatically, nor can any of the creatures that inhabit it. Israel's doxology knows that it is the gift of the wind of God that creates (see Gen. 1:2), that renews the face of the ground (Ps. 104:30). It is no surprise at all that the psalmist, singing for all those who gladly trust God's abundance, knows that praise defines human creaturely existence:

> I will sing to the LORD as long as I live;
>     I will sing praise to my God while I have being.
>                                               Ps. 104:33

It is no wonder that Psalm 145 ends with a similar doxology:

> My mouth will speak the praise of the LORD,
>     and all flesh will bless his holy name forever and ever.
>                                               Ps. 145:21

Doxology is the rhetoric of overflowing in which the words of awe and astonishment tumble out. The words are not to be uttered to an abstract principle or to an empty sky. They are words back to the limitless generosity of God who gives seed and bread:

> For as the rain and snow come down from heaven,
>     and do not return there until they have watered the earth,

     making it bring forth and sprout,
        giving seed to the sower and bread to the eater.
                                Isa. 55:10

The push of doxology beyond human speech in the natural world is a response matching the miracle of creation.

In church practice none has known this more fully than Francis of Assisi, who could ponder the doxology of all creation:

     Thou burning sun with golden beam,
     thou silver moon with softer gleam . . .
     thou rushing wind that art so strong,
     ye clouds that sail in heaven along,
     thou rising morn, in praise rejoice,
     ye lights of evening, find a voice!
     Thou fruitful earth that day by day
     unfoldest blessing on our way,
     the flowers and fruits that in thee grow,
     let them God's glory also show.

The refrain is "Alleluia, alleluia, alleluia, alleluia," a somewhat adjusted form of "Praise Yah." That phrase, an imperative summons, cannot be repeated too often, for what else could a rushing wind or a golden beam or a silver moon do? What else except to praise the Creator? It is all thanks for endless generosity!

## III

Doxology is about awed gratitude. It is response to gifts given by being in a posture of receptivity. That is why we sing such songs best with our hands outstretched. It is for good reason, then, that the creation liturgy in Genesis 1 culminates in Sabbath rest (Gen. 2:2–3). The world, as given by God, is not a restless, seething organism of recalcitrance. The world is "very good" as a fruit-bearing process to the benefit of all creatures. For that reason, at the center of biblical faith—indeed at the center of doxology—is the command to Sabbath rest. One can judge that Sabbath rest is the defining mark of God's grateful creatures, who rely on the Creator's generosity. Imagine: God rests! God is not anxious about creation working well. God is not a workaholic. More than that, Exodus 31:17 declares that Sabbath rest for God allowed God to recover God's very self, God's *nephesh*. The phrase translated there as "was refreshed" is a verbal use of the term *nephesh* ("soul" or "self"), so that God was "re-*nepheshed*," given life back after depletion. The wonder is that God, even God, is depleted and fatigued by the work of creation, so that Sabbath is recovery from depletion.

It is remarkable enough to imagine a depleted God who requires Sabbath. It is equally remarkable to ponder human persons who are depleted and who require recovery and restoration. Thus Sabbath breaks the grip of feverish work in the world, feverish accumulation. Big-time accumulators never take Sabbath rest. It is hard to imagine Pharaoh taking Sabbath rest. So of course Pharaoh is more and more depleted, and consequently more and more anxious. It is, in like manner, hard to imagine a conventional US consumer taking a Sabbath break from restless efforts at accumulation, performed for the sake of the children or the career or the church or whatever. It is hard to imagine the vicious cycle of anxiety being broken, but such is the wondrous reality of Sabbath rest, which is in sync with the rhythm of creation.[3] On that day, the pay-off day of creation, human persons join God and the birds and the lilies, and all creatures of our God and king and live in astonished abundance in order to ponder and experience and enjoy the abundance given by God. Sabbath is possible because God is known to guarantee what is needed to satisfy the desire of every living thing. Sabbath is a performance of an alternative to assert among ourselves that we are not pressed by scarcity, we are not consumed by anxiety, we are not driven by greed, and we are not available for anxious accumulation. At Sabbath, the creation takes into account the assured reality that "loaves abound." It turns out that abundance is not a matter of quantity. It is, rather, about being receptive rather than on the make, being a glad creature, rather than posturing as the creator of our own lives.

## IV

The convergence of *creation as fruitful food production*, response in *exuberant doxology* that matches God's abundance, and *restful Sabbath* to savor the abundance generates a venue for food sharing in gratitude and food eating in astonishment. That is the truth of the world that Israel confesses that decisively impacts our food production, food distribution, and food consumption.

In the purview of Israel Pharaoh, the accumulator, had skewed the entire process:

- Pharaoh, in his monopoly, has imagined that he, and *not the Creator*, is the one who provides food (see Ezek. 29:3).
- Pharaoh, in his scarcity, has *reduced the doxologies* of Israel to pained laments (see Exod. 2:23).
- Pharaoh, in his insatiable appetite, has gotten rid of all Sabbath rest (see Exod. 5:4–19).

*The annulment* of generous creation, *the silencing* of doxology, and *the termination* of Sabbath rest have resulted in a process of food production, food distribution, and food consumption that is unbearable for Israel and for the world.

For that reason, the exodus narrative is about the departure of Israel from the food system of Pharaoh. The narrative concerns Israel's coming to consciousness about its unbearable status in the food monopoly. Israel becomes an agent in its own history, rather than the recipient of what Pharaoh chooses to dole out. Israel breaks the silence of pain long denied, imagines an alternative existence outside the monopoly of Pharaoh, and dares to go there. The exodus narrative of course features Pharaoh the accumulator, who has skewed creation, and Moses, who is a daring and uncompromising leader. Most of all, it spectacularly features the Creator God, YHWH, who is the great adversary of Pharaoh, the accumulator. The contest between God and Pharaoh, between Moses (and Aaron) and the imperial magicians, is a food fight, a contest between theories and practices of food.

As the story continues, Israel departs the food monopoly of the accumulator. In Exodus 15, they are filled with exuberance and pause to sing and dance about the possibility of a new land that lies beyond the reach of Pharaoh's food policies (15:1–18, 20–21). Then they have to make their way into the wilderness, which in the Bible is a place without viable life supports or reliable food supplies. Their exuberance promptly fades. Just two verses into the wilderness, they are vexed and contentious; they wish they had never left the regime of the accumulator:

The whole congregation of the Israelites complained against Moses and Aaron in the wilderness. The Israelites said to them, "If only we had died by the hand of the LORD in the land of Egypt, when we sat by the fleshpots and ate our fill of bread; for you have brought us out into this wilderness to kill this whole assembly with hunger." (Exod. 16:2–3)

They thought they were going to die, and so they remembered the "meat pots" in the land of the accumulator that now looked better than the hunger of the wilderness. Indeed, in another reading of the same memory, they could recall in some detail the menu that they had enjoyed in Egypt:

If only we had meat to eat! We remember the fish we used to eat in Egypt for nothing, the cucumbers, the melons, the leeks, the onions, and the garlic; but now our strength is dried up; and there is nothing at all but this manna to look at. (Num. 11:4–6)

They did not at the moment remember the burden of their labor, only that they had food. And now, they are bereft. There is a reason that this story is preoccupied with the accumulator!

In the narrative that follows, they were surprised—and we are surprised in reading—that the wilderness turned out to be a place where YHWH could and would give gifts. Thus the Creator promises meat in the wilderness:

At twilight you shall eat meat. (Exod. 16:12)

And they got quail:

In the evening quails came up and covered the camp. (v. 13)

Before long they complained about the lack of water, and they got water:

But the people thirsted there for water; and the people complained against Moses and said, "Why did you bring us out of Egypt, to kill us and our children and livestock with thirst?" . . . The LORD said to Moses, "Go on ahead of the people, and take some of the elders of Israel with you; take in your hand the staff with which you struck the Nile, and go. I will be standing there in front of you on the rock at Horeb. Strike the rock, and water will come out of it, so that the people may drink." Moses did so, in the sight of the elders of Israel. (17:3, 5–6)

And in between the meat and the water, God promised bread:

In the morning you shall have your fill of bread. (16:12)

When it came in the morning, it was indeed bread; but it was not like any bread they had ever experienced. They were astonished and bewildered. They said in their surprise, "What is it?" In Hebrew they said, *man hu'*, that is, "manna." The wondered about it and knew it was "wonder bread" sent by God when they did not expect it to be given in the wilderness. They were given bread outside Pharaoh's monopoly. We are told only that it was, "a fine flaky substance, as fine as frost on the ground" (16:14). Moses clarified:

It is the bread that the LORD has given you to eat. (v. 15)

So now, in its bereavement, Israel has meat, water, and bread. They have all the essentials, even in the wilderness. They saw in that moment that the Creator God has the capacity to transform wilderness into creation, to transpose the place of hunger into a venue for abundance.

But the narrative does not move to a big theological claim. It remains with the concreteness of bread for the hungry. Moses, manager of the new bread, authorizes a harvest of the surprising bread:

Gather as much of it as each of you needs, an omer to a person according to the number of persons, all providing for those in their own tents. (16:16)

The bread was such a contrast to the bread of scarcity in Egypt, for there was enough. There was no scarcity of bread in the wilderness:

The Israelites did so, some gathering more, some less. But when they measured it with an omer, those who gathered much had nothing over, and those who gathered little had no shortage; they gathered as much as each of them needed. (vv. 17–18)

The generous Creator God had indeed "satisfied the desire of every living thing," so that the narrative echoes the doxological thanks of the Psalms.

There is only one catch:

Let no one leave any of it over until morning. (v. 19)

They cannot store it up, build a surplus, or hoard it. In this way the bread is so unlike the bread of the accumulator, for the one thing not to be done now is accumulate. But, says the narrator, they did not listen; they tried to save it up. The reason is that they feared scarcity. And the reason they feared scarcity is that they were completely inured to Pharaonic ideology of scarcity and anxiety, and so were propelled to accumulate.

But they could not do it. This bread would not permit surplus! The gifts of God do not lend themselves to accumulation.

> The bread got worms;
>    The bread began to smell badly;
> The bread melted (vv. 20–21).

On all counts, there was no way to save it up. No possibility of accumulation. No chance to confuse this bread with the bread of Pharaoh, which falls into monopoly, exclusion, hoarding, and eventually violence with hunger.

In verses 22–23 Moses makes a Friday exception to the rule of no storage, authorizing them to gather more bread on Friday, to have bread for Sabbath Saturday, when they are not to gather:

> "Tomorrow is a day of solemn rest, a holy sabbath to the LORD; bake what you want to bake and boil what you want to boil, and all that is left over put aside to be kept until morning." So they put it aside until morning, as Moses commanded them; and it did not become foul, and there were no worms in it. Moses said, "Eat it today, for today is a sabbath to the LORD; today you will not find it in the field. Six days you shall gather it; but on the seventh day, which is a sabbath, there will be none." (vv. 23–26)

Imagine that! Even in the wilderness where they feared scarcity, they are to prepare for Sabbath rest. They are to cease from their eager effort to secure bread. They are to pause to ponder that even there in the wilderness, creation functions. The Creator is alive and well. The bread holds for today, even as it multiplies enough for tomorrow when it is Sabbath.

This is a remarkable story. It is impossible to overstate its importance for Israel's memory and its significance for our perception of the food fight that offers an alternative to Pharaoh's hungry drive for monopoly. In this remarkable narrative, all the juices of the *garden* have been transferred to and activated in the *wilderness*. Wherever the glory of God appears, wilderness is transposed. There is no limit to the transformative power of YHWH, which contrasts to the impotence of Pharaoh. For that reason, Israel has doxologies about the transformative power of the Creator (see, e.g., Isa. 35:1–2; 41:17–20). Pharaoh assumed that the world was a closed system with no new gifts to be given. Israel's doxologies contradict that notion with the lyrical conviction that God has more gifts to give; those gifts are to be given in places where we think it is not possible to have new life. The manna narrative contradicts the ideology of Pharaoh! And the people of God have lived from the truth of that narrative ever since.

## V

The food fight is not resolved in the Old Testament but continues into the New Testament. There the challenge is not Pharaoh or Nebuchadnezzar but the imperial option of Rome, and the way that some Jews, notably the influential priests, colluded with imperial appetites. They did so by "fencing the table" with rules of holiness that carried with them rules of power and access.

It was the vocation of Jesus to exhibit and perform the abundance of God's rule that constituted a stark contrast to the ideology of parsimony that evoked the imperial rules of power and excess. In the horizon of Jesus, there was no ground for scarcity, and so no reason for anxiety, and so no need for accumulation, and so no pressure toward monopoly. Almost everything Jesus did in his teaching and in his action challenged those rules and brought him into conflict with the authorities. He joined the food fight as a "transgressor" of the conventional rules of food. Thus at the beginning of Mark, the issue is joined:

And as he sat at dinner in Levi's house, many tax collectors and sinners were also sitting with Jesus and his disciples—for there were many who followed him. When the scribes of the Pharisees saw that he was eating with sinners and tax collectors, they said to his disciples, "Why does he eat with tax collectors and sinners?" When Jesus heard this, he said to them, "Those who are well have no need of a physician, but those who are sick; I have come to call not the righteous but sinners." (Mark 2:15–17)

Already in Mark 2:1–12, he runs into opposition, for his willingness to heal and his capacity to forgive are acts of gracious generosity in a theological world that is governed by parsimony. By his readiness to eat with the "disqualified," he makes clear that the food supply of the Creator is not limited to those who keep the rules of holiness and power; in fact, the food supply is sufficient to be distributed "indiscriminately." Indeed, his entry into the synagogue to begin his public life features a declaration of Jubilee by quoting from Isaiah 61:1 (Luke 4:18–19). The Jubilee of course is the most subversive and dangerous teaching in the Bible, for it enacts a different kind of entitlement that pays no heed to conventional rules of distribution and property.[4]

In Luke 14, Jesus is challenged about rules for Sabbath keeping (vv. 1–6). This is followed by a narrative about "places of honor" at a dinner, which opens the way for his parable about dinner, for he understood that rules for dining reflect power arrangements in society. He reflects on who gets to eat and who decides who gets to eat.

> But when you give a banquet, invite the poor, the crippled, the lame, and the blind. And you will be blessed, because they cannot repay you, for you will be repaid at the resurrection of the righteous. (vv. 13–14)

This dictum about inclusive sharing is an introduction to his parable of the great banquet about food for street people:

> Go out at once into the streets and lanes of the town and bring in the poor, the crippled, the blind, and the lame. . . . Go out into the roads and lanes, and compel people to come in, so that my house may be filled. (vv. 21, 23)

His story envisions a great offer of food with proper honor and concern for all the members of the community, without reference to qualification.

Alongside his words, Jesus' actions push the food fight to greater extremity. In Mark 6:30–44 he is in a "deserted place," that is, a "wilderness." He observes the hungry crowd, has "compassion for them," and distributes food without attention to qualification. He takes what little food is available in the crowd and performs and makes available the abundance of God's new creation. In Jesus, the new creation of God's abundance is again visible in the wilderness. The convergence of "wilderness" and "compassion" makes clear that Jesus is reiterating the manna narrative of Exodus 16. He brings food where there is none. His actions consist in

- taking the five loaves
- blessing the loaves
- breaking the loaves
- giving the loaves for distribution

The narrative does not explain or exhibit any curiosity about how this could happen. It does not invite, require, or even permit explanation. It is enough that Jesus transforms that "deserted place" into a place of well-being for "five thousand men." I suppose we are permitted to add the accompanying women and children. There was enough, more than enough, left over for twelve baskets of bread.

In Mark 8:1–10, he is again in the "desert." He again comes to a great crowd without anything to eat. He again has compassion. He again enacts the abundance of the new creation:

- He takes the loaves.
- He gives thanks for what bread he has.
- He breaks the loaves.
- He gives them to his disciples for distribution.

There was, again, more than enough. The crowd numbered four thousand, and seven baskets of bread were surplus this time.

This twice-told story about this twice-performed wonder lies outside the grip of anxious monopoly. Jesus is no accumulator. He relies on the bread that is at hand. He passes it all out because it is needed for the hungry crowd; he knew and trusted that there would be more as it was needed. It is clear that when Jesus comes as the agent of the new creation of God, there is no scarcity, and so no anxiety, and so no accumulation. The narrative shows the way in which the food fight is to be resolved: by the embrace of the new creation of abundance that refuses frantic production, that eschews parsimonious distribution, and that allows for consumption that fills but does not overwhelm. Indeed, it is impossible to imagine anyone in either crowd overeating on that day!

These two episodes in the food fight are the epitome of the message and ministry of Jesus and the sum of the "good news" that the force of God's abundance has broken the power of fearful parsimony. It is no wonder that in the narrative of Mark, the second episode is followed by a session of critical reflection, for his own disciples do not discern what he has done any more than do the Pharisees. His disciples are in a boat without bread. Well, there is "one loaf" (Mark 8:14), which some think refers to Jesus himself as the bread of life. Jesus warns his disciples about the junk food of those who make the rules of access:

Watch out—beware of the yeast of the Pharisees and the yeast of Herod. (v. 15)

Then he asks them to reflect on what he has done in supplying abundant food. He asks them for discernment, of which they are incapable:

Do you still not perceive or understand? Are your hearts hardened? Do you have eyes, and fail to see? Do you have ears, and fail to hear? And do you not remember? (vv. 17–18)

They do not respond to his questions, and they likely avoid eye contact with him. They do not understand that the terrain of the food fight has, by his presence and his action, decisively shifted. They are completely oblivious.

Like any good teacher, Jesus retreats from such large and challenging questions back to a concrete operational question:

When I broke the five loaves for the five thousand, how many baskets full of broken pieces did you collect? (v. 19)

The answer confidently: "Twelve."

And the seven for the four thousand, how many baskets full of broken pieces did you collect? (v. 20)

They answer promptly: "Seven." There is a long pause. The disciples are relieved that they have survived the quiz. But Jesus sees what he has on his hands. He has eager disciples who are good at concrete operational data. They know the statistics. But they have no idea what they have witnessed. They completely miss the point, that a new reality about food and hunger is now before their very eyes. And so he asks his disciples:

Do you not yet understand? (v. 21)

He says it, perhaps whimsically, surely with disappointment, maybe a tone of rebuke. But this is how it is among us characteristically, as followers of Jesus. The new disclosure is too radical and revolutionary, and we cannot take it in. Because what is exhibited is the fact that the old categories of the food fight are now irrelevant. The old patterns of Pharaoh are obsolete, because that old pattern cannot engage in generous sharing. The new creation is a gift that keeps on giving, and there is no excuse now for parsimony toward the neighbor.

Mark offers a hint of the reason for the disciples' obtuseness:

They did not understand about the loaves, but their hearts were hardened. (Mark 6:52)

The phrase "hearts were hardened" clearly alludes to the exodus narrative. Pharaoh refused to let the slaves go because he had a hard heart (see Exod. 7:22; 8:19; 9:35). His hard heart made him anxious. Consequently he needed more granaries for more accumulation, which in turn required slave labor. His hard heart caused him to misunderstand the emancipatory reality of God.

And now the disciples think like Pharaoh and are, like him, enthralled by notions of scarcity. What an amazing summary of our problem! The disciples miss the reality of God's abundant bread because they perceive reality in the categories of Pharaoh. Well, so say we all! All of us, give or take a little, are propelled by nightmares of scarcity that are blind and resistant to the truth of divine generosity that pervades creation. In fact the good news is that this food fight is over. But we keep reenacting and reiterating our ancient and abiding loyalty to the mistaken categories of Pharaoh. We order our lives and our communities, and we build our policies of food and money and credit and war and supplies on the basis of scarcity. And we do so, even when we have seen otherwise!

## VI

To this breathtaking new world of Jesus, I add only one note from Paul. In his ethical inventory for the new life in Christ, he writes:

> Contribute to the needs of the saints; extend hospitality to strangers. (Rom. 12:13)

He underscores the two virtues of abundance: generosity and hospitality (see 12:8). But in 2 Corinthians 8, he brings his conviction about generosity to concrete practice by making a strong appeal for the church in Corinth to contribute generously to the fund to support the church in Jerusalem. It is a bid for generosity, grounded in Christology:

> For you know the generous act of our Lord Jesus Christ, that though he was rich, yet for your sakes he became poor, so that by his poverty you might become rich. (2 Cor. 8:9)

Paul goes to great lengths not to command but only to persuade by being reasonable:

> I do not mean that there should be relief for others and pressure on you, but it is a question of a fair balance between your present abundance and their need, so that their abundance may be for your need, in order that there may be a fair balance. (vv. 13–14)

And then, most astonishingly, in the interest of the "fair balance between your present abundance and their need," he quotes Exodus 16:18:

> The one who had much did not have too much,
>      and the one who had little did not have too little.
>                                                    2 Cor. 8:15

Paul alludes to the manna narrative to urge sharing with others, grounded in the conviction that there is more than enough for everyone. It is all about generosity that is funded by the prior generosity of God, who satisfies the desire and need of every living thing.

## VII

The news of an alternative gives us a new way to participate in the food fight. The news is of a new creation, enacted by Jesus, that keeps on giving in ways that make parsimony obsolete. The church's dramatic enactment of that new settlement of the food fight is the Eucharist, in which we reiterate the four great verbs of Jesus in the wilderness: "take, bless, break, give." Imagine having a regular ritual called "*Thanks*"! This *thank-meal* is an act of defiance, a refusal of Pharaoh's system of accumulation, a resolve to live

- from *abundance* and not scarcity,
- in *trust* and not anxiety,
- by *sharing* and not accumulating,
- for *neighborly covenant* and not monopoly.

We are left with the question of whether, in a world of fearful parsimony and violent struggle to corner the market on food, the abundance is true and reliable. Well, we have already signed on for it. The truth of abundance follows from Easter, in which the power of death has been exposed as a fraud. Our task is to connect the dots between our big affirmation, "Christ is risen; he is risen indeed," and policies and practices of food production, distribution, and consumption.

The claim has immediate implications for how we eat, how much we eat, and with whom we eat. It has long-term implications for policy, because a bloated military budget is based on a fetish of accumulation. The people who are grounded in the generous abundance of God's new creation are the ones who will, perhaps in time, dismantle the entire system of anxiety and greed that feeds hostility. It is our conviction that the new creation is reliable and will feed us until we want no more. Jesus broke down abundance to its most elemental components:

I was hungry and you gave me food, I was thirsty and you gave me something to drink. . . . I was hungry and you gave me no food, I was thirsty and you gave me nothing to drink. (Matt. 25:35, 42)

The great news is that we no longer need to be on the hopeless, losing side in the food fight!

## Questions for Reflection

1. What table prayers do you know or say regularly? How do your table prayers function as an ongoing conversation with God and/or a reminder of the "other way" of approaching food and hunger in an anxious world?

2. Where and when do you find "Sabbath rest" that reminds you to trust in God's generosity and provision, instead of the pressure to work, be productive, and accumulate?

3. How do you see the story of quail, manna, and water in the wilderness as a narrative at work in your own life? When and where do you need to recall that "God has more gifts to give; those gifts are to be given in places where we think it is not possible to have new life" (p. 35)?

4. Brueggemann says, "The people who are grounded in the generous abundance of God's new creation are the ones who will, perhaps in time, dismantle the entire system of anxiety and greed that feeds hostility" (p. 41). Where do you see movement toward this new future in your own community? What role does the Eucharist or communion meal play in your participation in it?

Chapter 3

# To Whom Does the Land Belong?

$A$s we have seen, grace in the Bible characteristically interrupts and overcomes insecurities stemming from the threat of scarcity. Furthermore, considerations of grace and parsimony, scarcity and abundance, are always shaped by conceptions of creation. The pragmatic question concerning creation is not evolution or "intelligent design," but who owns, governs, and guarantees the earth. The question is made concrete and urgent when we remember that the Hebrew word "earth" (*'erets*) is most often translated "land." Thus the creation question is *"Who has a right to the land?"*

I

I begin with three biblical texts that ponder that issue. The most familiar is the doxological beginning of Psalm 24: "The earth is the LORD's and all that is in it." The Hebrew begins: *la–YHWH ha–'arets,* and so we can see that the earth/land is *'erets,* and the owner is YHWH, indicated by a possessive preposition *la–*. The land belongs to YHWH! What follows in the psalm concerning this "King of glory" is an ethic that is congruent with the "owner" (Ps. 24:3–6). The psalm concerns a ritual entry by YHWH into the temple to enact and dramatize YHWH's gracious proprietorship of the land.

The same claim is made in Hosea, wherein the prophet anticipates that disobedient Israel will be expelled from "the land of YHWH" and placed under control of hostile superpowers:

> They shall not remain in the land of the LORD;
> but Ephraim shall return to Egypt,
> and in Assyria they shall eat unclean food.
>
> Hos. 9:3

Again the Hebrew is *'erets YHWH*. It is assumed that the land belongs to YHWH and must therefore be organized and governed according to YHWH's will and character. Israel has violated that will and therefore cannot remain as YHWH's beloved people.

The issue is formulated differently in 2 Samuel 3:12, wherein Abner puts a defiant chiding rhetorical question to David: "To whom does the land belong" (*lemi–'erets*)? Again the land is *'erets* and the possessive pronoun is the same as in Psalm 24:1. Only here the issue from Abner to David is whether the land (the territory of north Israel) should be controlled by David or left to the remnant of Saul's enterprise. As the strongest of Saul's party, Abner is proposing to cede the land over to David—for a price. Thus Abner's question is a cynical one that appeals to David's rough-and-tumble aspirations for political advancement.

What strikes one most is that Abner (or the narrator) has completely forgotten Israel's doxological liturgies that regularly acknowledge that the land belongs to YHWH, the Creator. Abner reckons only that the land either *belongs to David* or *belongs to Saul*. When the question is posed in that cynical way—as it most often is posed in "the real world"—the claim of YHWH and the derivative claim of proper governance are readily and easily driven from the horizon. The calculating challenge of Abner to David is of interest and importance because the question of Abner—rather than a liturgical theology of creation—most often dictates political, economic, and military policy, and a self-serving sense of entitlement in the world. Thus I propose to consider *creation faith* around the urgent questions of ownership, control, and governance of the land and its natural resources.[1]

When the Creator God is eliminated from the question of land/creation, then the land question is characteristically resolved—as Abner assumed—on the basis of *power*, without any question about *legitimacy*. Thus in large scope it is fair to say that the story of ownership, control, and governance of the land is a narrative of *strength* against *vulnerability*:

- The strong characteristically claim land and resources that belong to the weak;
- white Western nations, since the fifteenth century and in the name of missionaries-cum-colonialism, have claimed what belongs to indigenous peoples;
- men have characteristically claimed what belongs to women;
- the developed powers with enormous technological advantage have claimed what "underdeveloped" powers cannot defend for themselves.

The story of the land is a story of power, confiscation, and usurpation that is rooted in a crass sense of entitlement. Wherever some are able to enjoy the outcomes of shameless power, the entitlement is most often cast in well-sounding cadences of legitimacy.

## II

Amid that enactment of *shameless power* with *cadences of legitimacy*, biblical faith asserts YHWH as Creator, a claim that makes all human claims to the land penultimate. The church's confession of "God as Creator" stands first in the Bible and in the creeds. The church, in its confession of "God as Creator," asserts that the earth (land) is not an autonomous commodity, a freestanding entitlement; it is not, moreover, an available commodity to be taken in a crapshoot or divided by lots, as was his "seamless" garment (Ps. 22:18; see John 19:23). It is rather a creature of YHWH, well beloved and cared for by the Creator, blessed (Gen. 1:22), looked over (Deut. 11:12), and regularly renewed in generativity and fruitfulness.

Human utilization and enjoyment of the land and its resources come under the rubric of "love of God." Indeed the command to love God "with all your heart, and with all your soul, and with all your might" (Deut. 6:5) is designed precisely for entry into the land:

> Now this is the commandment—the statutes and the ordinances—
> that the LORD your God charged me to teach you to observe in the
> land that you are about to cross into and occupy, so that you and
> your children and your children's children may fear the LORD your
> God all the days of your life, and keep all his decrees and his com-
> mandments that I am commanding you, so that your days may be

long. Hear therefore, O Israel, and observe them diligently, so that
it may go well with you, and so that you may multiply greatly in
a land flowing with milk and honey, as the LORD, the God of your
ancestors, has promised you. (Deut. 6:1–3)

Love of God correlates with occupation of land; consequently, *love
of God* means to *order the land* in ways that are congruent with
YHWH's character; this character, we know everywhere in Scripture, is marked by graciousness, mercy, steadfast love, compassion,
fidelity, generosity, and forgiveness.

And of course if we characterize the proper ordering of land in
such covenantal ways, it follows that the way we may "love God"
in land-as-creation is to love neighbor, for finally we have no other
way to love God (1 John 4:20–21). Thus our love of God is to order
the land for the sake of the common good. We may then articulate
dramatic lines of the land ethic in Scripture:

> The land belongs to YHWH.
> The mandate is to love God in the land.
> We may love God in the land by loving the neighbor.

The land, its potential for power, and its resources are to be devoted
to the *common good*, that *all the neighbors* are to enjoy the fruitfulness and well-being of land as God's creation.

## III

That remarkable and central biblical claim about creation/land is
the primary point of proclamation in the church that is rooted
squarely in the creeds. It is a most elemental claim of faith that
now needs insistent voicing. But in recent times, the church has
largely forfeited its capacity for such proclamation. On one hand,
that forfeiture is due to the church's endless and disproportionate
preoccupation with "sin and salvation" of a privatistic kind. On
the other hand, the forfeiture is due to a commitment to "God's
mighty deeds in history," as though God were known in dramatic
events, to the exclusion of the slow, steady, steadfast ordering of
lived reality.[2]

The church's forfeiture of this crucial dimension of faith on both counts has left the issue of land outside the horizon of preaching, and has left our understanding of land in the categories of modern Enlightenment possessiveness.[3] Lynn White once infamously claimed that the Genesis text on "dominion" was the root of land domination and exploitation in the world (Gen. 1:28).[4] That connection has now been discredited and shown to be a careless and massive overreading of the text. It is not the Bible but modern Enlightenment philosophy—rooted in Bacon, Descartes, and Locke—that offered the modern Western world a notion of land as *absolute possession and property.*[5] Without the claim of a vigorous God articulated in political idiom, the land has been readily handed over to human possession and exploitation, whether under divine kings in the seventeenth century, nation-states in the eighteenth century, military superpowers in the nineteenth and twentieth centuries, or the superrich in gated communities in the twenty-first century. Once the claim of the Creator God has been sidelined, the sense of human entitlement may stretch in the contemporary world all the way from private consumer desires to aggressive imperial pursuits. The inevitable outcome is a loss of the common good, and a refusal to finance through taxes an infrastructure that will keep life livable, because taxes take away from private self-aggrandizing.

The preacher, so I suggest, is placed as a witness and advocate for *land as creation* in a society that is ideologically committed to *land as possession.* The preacher is summoned to a contestation that is enormously difficult, precisely because both private entitlement and national-corporate aggression are rooted in an ideology that remains unexposed and unrecognized, even though diametrically opposed to the church's creed concerning the Creator God and Christ, in whom "all things hold together" (Col. 1:17). Indeed, there is no category in that alien ideology for any common good, the very "good" that is the intent of the Creator, and so all things fall apart in the service of private good.

## IV

This ideology of private possession, in denial of the Creator and at the expense of the neighbor, has been given its classic expression in Enlightenment thought, wherein the European intelligentsia managed to purge the claims of the biblical God from their horizon.[6] But the ideology itself is much, much older, even as it has reached virulent form in the contemporary world. This ideology of private possession permeates the thinking of liberals and conservatives who have never heard of Bacon or Locke, relying rather on the uncritical declarations of pundits and politicians on the right and left alike. This ideology is pervasive, enhanced by the consumerism of the relentless liturgies of television.

Consequently, when the preacher begins to talk about creation as God's ownership, control, and governance of the land, the preacher heads directly into a most deeply held and largely unrecognized and uncriticized alternative. The task of preaching, for that reason, is as urgent as it is risky. In what follows I will list four examples of that ideology and then cite three modest concrete signs of an alternative around which the preacher may stake a claim. Here are four clear examples of the ideology of private possession against which creation faith makes its testimony, four ways to disturb creation and vex the gracious Creator to whom the land belongs:

1. The *exercise of eminent domain*, whereby the powerful, with smart lawyers, seize the "inheritance" of the vulnerable. The narrative of 1 Kings 21 is a case study in such socioeconomic disruption. King Ahab wants the property of Naboth for a vegetable garden and promises Naboth appropriate compensation (v. 2). The narrative turns on the voiced vocabulary of Ahab and Naboth, terms that bespeak rival theories of economics and competing notions of land as creation. Ahab regards the land as a "possession," a commodity for buying and selling and trading—one piece of land is as good as another. Naboth, by contrast, speaks of "ancestral inheritance" to which he is intrinsically and inalienably attached (v. 3). Behind this notion of ancestral inheritance is the large vision of the Jubilee, a provision that makes no sense unless there is a commitment to protect ancestral property. In this contest between rival land theories, the powerful, as usual, will prevail. In Naboth's old peasant presupposition, ancestral land is not only inviolate but in fact pertains to the very ordering of creation.[7] It need hardly be added that the king's promise to compensate Naboth was not forthcoming, even as a promised compensation for the exercise of eminent domain in the

Atlanta Olympics in 1996 was not forthcoming. Those who regard land as a tradable commodity tend to have amnesia about long-term neighborly loyalty.

2. *Confiscation*. The narrative case here is in 2 Kings 8:1–6. A woman, the one whose son had died and was raised to new life by Elisha (2 Kgs. 4:8–37), had fled the land in the face of an acute famine. But of course the practice of confiscating economics did not cease in her absence. When she returned, she discovered she had lost her house and her field (2 Kgs. 8:3). There is no suggestion that the loss was illegal or immoral, just the normal working of the economy.

In her loss she "appealed" to the king. The verb is to "cry out," the desperate strategy of the vulnerable who announce in loud ways the suffering inflicted by the working of the powerful (see Luke 18:1–8). The woman addresses her appeal to the king, who has the capacity to redress such confiscation and to return to her what is hers. We do not know why the king honors her appeal, as kings often do not. Perhaps this king, son of Ahab, has learned something by a study of the narrative of Naboth's vineyard; or perhaps he is under the influence of Elisha through Gehazi, in whose presence he receives the appeal. Either way, the king acts to *restore* what is rightly hers. The narrative attests that what the powerful are capable of taking is not in any case legitimate. This odd narrative attests that under the pressure of prophetic tradition, the ruling class can on occasion curb and redress confiscation, and so return land management to its proper shape.

3. *Usurpation*. The prophetic oracle of Micah 2:1–5 is an important marker in Old Testament teaching about the land that belongs to YHWH. The oracle begins with "woe" (NRSV "alas"), which means "big trouble coming" in the normal workings of the order of creation. The indictment voiced by the prophet concerns sharp land dealings whereby the strong usurp the property of the weak. Micah, an agrarian protestor, has great suspicion about big-time urban operators who connive at night "on their beds," phone their agents at daybreak, and by noon have seized property. This action is apparently fully legal, but it violates the neighborhood and upsets the ordering of the land economy.[8]

The operational word in the prophetic oracle is "covet," which here does not refer to petty envy but to policies and practices of economic acquisitiveness that are, in a commodity-driven society, uncurbed.

The target of such acquisitiveness is houses and fields (Mic. 2:2), the same word pair used to describe the loss of the woman in 2 Kings 8:3. Micah the poet, moreover, refers to house and field as "inheritance," the tribal domain that is inalienable but now is usurped by acquisitive policy and practice that no longer honor old neighborly notions of the land. It is no wonder that the oracle of Micah continues with a harsh "therefore" of judgment in 2:3, anticipating a time to come when those who rapaciously seize the land of vulnerable neighbors are themselves vexed when YHWH "alters the inheritance of my people" (v. 4). Now the shift in "inheritance" concerns not just a few rural neighbors but the whole of the land economy by foreign intervention. The oracle concludes in verse 5 with anticipation of a new "casting of lines" for land distribution, an assembly at the courthouse in which the "coveters" will be excluded from the new land management!

4. *Arrogant autonomy*. The three cases I have cited all refer to small local transactions wherein the urban commodity economy displaces the old tribal economy of inheritance, a displacement that characteristically goes under the rubric of "development." In citing Ezekiel 29:3–7, I move from conventional tribal conflict to the heady world of uncurbed superpowers. In the Old Testament, "Egypt" (along with Babylon) is a cipher for superpower pretension and posturing that assumes no theocentric limit to power. The upshot of the oracle of Ezekiel is that when Judah turns to Egypt for help against Babylon, Judah will find Egypt to be a mere "staff of reed" with a broken body, that is, nothing more than totally unreliable weakness (vv. 6–7).

Our interest, however, is in the indictment of Egypt in verse 3, wherein the arrogant empire is condemned for saying, via its policies, "My Nile is my own; I made it for myself." Everyone knows that the Nile was there before Egypt, that the river is God's accomplishment, and that its reliability made Egyptian culture and power possible. But superpower arrogance has caused Pharaoh to misconstrue, and to invert the truth of creation. Rather than acknowledge that the Lord made the Nile that in turn made Egypt, Pharaoh can imagine he made the Nile. (The verb, *'asah*, is commonly used for creation.) Given that misconstrual, Egypt of course is not answerable to anyone, and so can use, abuse, exploit, distort, consume, and eventually destroy creation, because the river is the crown's personal property.

But the indictment of the prophetic oracle that follows rejects the imperial claim of autonomy. Readers and preachers of this text amid US superpower pretension will have little trouble transposing this oracle to "the last superpower" that imagines it can evoke "a new world order" to its own liking. Superpowers regularly refuse to learn about tenacious hold on the land that "colonies" continue to have, precisely because the land for them is never *possession* but always *inheritance*. It is for good reason that the prophets anticipate divine judgment on the superpower, a failed carcass to be fed to other creatures: "animals of the earth, birds of the air" (29:5). In the end, Egypt will learn that "I am the LORD," and that superpower status is fragile and penultimate (29:6).

These conventional ways of acquisitiveness—eminent domain, confiscation, usurpation, and arrogant autonomy—violate the land that belongs to YHWH and *not* to kings (1 Kgs. 21), *not* to commodity traders (2 Kgs. 8:1–6; Mic. 2:1–5), and *not* to rapacious superpowers (Ezek. 29:3).

## V

Alongside these harsh denunciations of uncurbed acquisitiveness, I finish by citing three affirmations about the earth as guaranteed by the Creator:

1. "The meek shall inherit the earth." This familiar teaching in the Sermon on the Mount (Matt. 5:5) is a quotation from Psalm 37:11, which is a sapiential meditation on the future of the land. Five times the psalm speaks of "inheriting the land." Alongside the "meek," it refers to "those who wait for the LORD" (Ps. 37:9), "the blessed by the LORD" (v. 22), "the righteous" (v. 39), and those who "keep to his way" (v. 34) as the ones who will inherit the land. These various phrases all refer to Torah obedience, to those who conduct their life according to the well-being of the neighborhood as willed by the gracious Creator who owns the land. The negative counterpoint in each case is "the wicked," those who advance themselves at the expense of the neighbor. This psalm, characteristic of wisdom teaching, attests that there are inviolate "givens" ordained in creation that cannot be safely transgressed. Among them is the maintenance of land through the practice of neighborliness.

2. The Decalogue, as is well known, concludes, "You shall not covet" (Exod. 20:17; Deut. 5:21), a commandment that refers in these two verses to wife, house, field, or "anything that belongs to your neighbor." It cannot be unimportant that this command that curbs acquisitiveness concludes the Decalogue and stands in the position of final accent. The verb "covet" is the same one used in the indictment of Micah 2:2 (and rendered in Gen. 3:6 as "desired"). The command and the prophetic indictment, as well as the creation narrative, understand that uncurbed desire will distort creation.[9] The commandment makes clear that, in the context of land management, not all that is possible is permissible.

3. In both Torah instruction and wisdom saying, the land inheritance of the vulnerable is inviolate:

> You must not move your neighbor's boundary marker, set up by former generations, on the property that will be allotted to you in the land that the LORD your God is giving you to possess. (Deut. 19:14)

> Do not remove an ancient landmark
>     or encroach on the fields of orphans,
> for their redeemer is strong;
>     he will plead their cause against you.
>                 Prov. 23:10–11; see 22:28

The teachers in Israel can imagine that life is ordered by the gracious Creator so that the strong and the weak may live together peaceably and justly. A violation of the entitlement of the vulnerable by any practice, legal or military, violates creation and brings death.

Creation faith in the Old Testament links together the will of the awesome Creator and the well-being of the most vulnerable. Creation faith makes our will to control and possess penultimate, which is no doubt why love of God the Creator regularly evolves into love of neighbor. Or, as the wisdom teacher has it,

> Those who mock the poor insult their Maker;
>     those who are glad at calamity will not go unpunished.
>                 Prov. 17:5

Such a connection may give us pause as citizens of an aggressive superpower. Such connection makes honest preaching hazardous against the ideology of possessive autonomy, but for all that reason no less urgent. Abner's question lingers: "To whom does the land belong?" Unlike Abner, we may entertain a reference point beyond the immediate conflict of "ours" and "theirs." Beyond any romanticism in Psalm 24:1, there is a starchy insistence upon another landowner who is full of grace and truth!

## Questions for Reflection

1. Where do you see the land and its resources near you being devoted to the common good, where all neighbors can enjoy the fruitfulness of God's creation? In what ways could this happen more intentionally, especially by the efforts of faith communities?

2. What current examples do you see for the conventional ways of acquisitiveness that forget that "the earth is the Lord's"—eminent domain, confiscation, usurpation, and arrogant autonomy?

3. How do you understand the commandment "You shall not covet" in relation to creation and idolatry?

4. How open is your faith community to preaching about creation faith? How can you help pave the way for such proclamation, witness, and advocacy?

# Chapter 4

# The Practice of Homefulness

*T*he Bible is just as concerned about shelter and housing as it is about food, as we saw in chapters 1 and 2, and the ordering of the land, as in chapter 3. It is my conviction that learning to reread the Bible is not only enormously interesting but also enormously urgent, for in rereading the Bible, we will be permitted to reread our social reality. This double rereading is important, I believe, because what we need in relation to the problem of homelessness is not information but courage, energy, will, freedom, and impetus. The latter will not come from socioeconomic, political analysis alone, important as such analysis is, but from our deepest texts, where we hear a voice of holiness that can intrude upon our settled senses of ourselves and our social reality. The church's task is thus urgent, because it can resituate the *homelessness* generated by our economy in a context of evangelical *homefulness*, as willed by God, and thereby cause us to see our crisis differently.

I

The first text I want to consider is Hosea 14:1–3, which issues Hosea's final invitation to repent:

> Return, O Israel, to the LORD your God,
> for you have stumbled because of your iniquity.
> Take words with you
> and return to the LORD;
> say to him,
> "Take away all guilt;

> accept that which is good,
>     and we will offer
>     the fruit of our lips.
> Assyria will not save us;
>     we will not ride upon horses;
> we will say no more, 'Our God,'
>     to the work of our hands.
> In you the orphan finds mercy."

The first line, "Return to the LORD," is reiterated in the second verse. The following verses answer the question, return from what?:

- return from iniquity, for you have stumbled into *false faith*;
- return from wrong speech, where you have embraced *self-deceptive ideology*,
- return from horses and Assyrians, *mistaken security* in arms,
- return from the work of our hands, *self-sufficiency*.

That is a lot to give up: false faith, deceptive ideology, mistaken security, self-sufficiency.

Nothing yet has been said to characterize YHWH, the one to whom return is to be made. Then comes the most important punch line: "In you the orphan finds mercy!" What a line! The statement has three phrases. *In you*, in the gracious God of Israel, the liberator of slaves, the giver of commandments, the patron of covenant, the provider of land. "In you" recalls and makes present the entire long history of YHWH, who cares about land, food, clothing, houses, material well-being.

The second phrase is *the orphan*. Remember, this text comes out of a tribal society with large, extended families with inheritance, genealogy, and patrimony. Everyone there has a place and belongs, is known and named and cared for . . . unless your daddy has died. The problem about being an orphan is not that you grieve over your dead parent. It is rather that you lose your place. If your father dies, you do not belong, you are without name, genealogy, patrimony, defense, rescue, advocate, avenger. You are always, everywhere, at risk and in jeopardy. That is how the world was ordered. And if we reflect long, we see that the realities of social power have not changed much. It is a high-risk deal to have lost your place in the world.

Thus in the first two phrases of this poetic line, we have an odd juxtaposition. There is YHWH, who has this long, faithful history of gracious intervention and provision, and there is the orphan, who has no name, no history, no prospect, no chance in the world. YHWH is the guarantor; the orphan is the one who has no guarantees.

Everything hinges on the third term of the poetic line: *finds mercy*, which is one of three primal terms for grace that are repeatedly associated with God in the Old Testament (see Exod. 34:6). It is in mercy, grace, and steadfast love that the guarantor and the one without guarantees get together. The two are linked in mercy that comes from YHWH and goes to the orphan. The term "mercy" denotes womblike mother love, gracious attentiveness and solidarity, fidelity that cuts underneath merit to give guarantees.[1] This is the one who gives guarantees for life to the one who has no guarantees for life. Thus, the entire rhetorical unit says, (a) leave false faith, deceptive ideology, mistaken security, and self-sufficiency; (b) get back in obedience to the one who gives guarantees to those who lack every guarantee. I suspect that this text will do for us both because of its powerful witness to God and because it is precisely such foundational repentance that is required if we are to have any serious housing revolution.

"Mercy to the orphan" is thus a fairly precise equivalent to "homes for the homeless," because the homeless are the orphans in our society, for they have no protective tribe. In such a context, "mercy" translates into "a house," which bespeaks membership in a protective community. Yet this marvelous text is open to an insidious misreading. Because mercy for the orphan, homes for the homeless, comes from YHWH, it is thus possible for us (even if we are dead wrong) to take the text as an invitation to quiescence and abdication, to conclude that God gives mercy to orphans, and that if God gives homes to the homeless, then homelessness is not our problem. And with a bad theology of otherworldliness, the church has often invited such a reading. When the Bible is read so transcendentally, then the human dimension of the housing crisis is cut off from our theological confession, and energy for the issues becomes difficult to sustain.

Thus we must work at serious rereading of the Bible, away from our transcendental naiveté. While *mercy* and *orphan* are clear enough in their meanings, what we have to work on is "in you," "*in YHWH*," the one to whom we are summoned to return. God talk is never simply transcendental, spiritual, and otherworldly, but always carries within it a tacit theory of social relations that is inherently laden with socioeconomic, political implications. And as a number of scholars have discerned, the specific character of YHWH is engaged in serious social criticism.[2]

Thus, when this text says, "Return to YHWH your God," and concludes by saying, "in you," in Hosea's Mosaic-prophetic faith, it belongs undeniably to the very character of YHWH—of Yahwism—to foster, advocate, and enact a certain social practice. That is, YHWH is not a God safely in heaven or in church; rather, YHWH is in fact a *specific social practice* that is taken seriously in obedient Israel. Returning to YHWH means returning to the social practice in which YHWH, YHWH's community, and YHWH's covenant are definitionally involved.

Consider the following line from Jeremiah, who learned so much from Hosea, as he describes King Josiah as a model for a good king:

> He judged the cause of the poor and needy;
>     then it was well.
> Is not this to know me?
>     says the LORD.
>
> Jer. 22:16

This extraordinary text shows how YHWH is understood in terms of social practice.[3] The text does not say that if one takes care of the poor and the needy, then that one will get to know YHWH. Nor does the text say that if one knows YHWH, then one will take care of the poor and needy. The two elements are synonymous, not sequential or related as cause and effect. Caring for the poor and needy is equivalent to knowing YHWH. YHWH is indeed a mode of social practice and a way of social relation.

Thus Jeremiah 22:16 illuminates Hosea 14:1–3. "Return to YHWH" means to return to the God who is present in social practice that is a sharp contrast to false faith, deceptive ideology, mistaken security, and self-sufficiency. The housing crisis among the orphans will not be solved by turning things over to a holy God in heaven, nor by heroic action on our part, but by increasing investment in the social practice wherein YHWH is present, a social practice that in every generation and every circumstance involves liberation and covenant, gifts and land, and that inevitably clashes with the status quo. Thus the housing problem, when construed according to the gospel, is an evangelical task that involves not only inviting more folks into the story and social practice defined by the character of this God, but also brings together our baptismal identities and the concrete practice of YHWH in giving guarantees to orphans. The prophetic alternative is always aimed against any separation between the transcendence of God and the social practice of God, that is, between word and flesh.

## II

With this framing program, "In you the orphan finds mercy" (Hos. 14:3), we may now lay out a taxonomy of YHWH's story of housing. This will highlight several crucial texts and show how they may be linked together in a coherent and authorizing sequence. I shall do so in three groups, which correspond to the three phases of ancient Israel's story. The first phase includes three texts that reflect on *the originary claim of having a house*. At the outset of its story, Israel assumes all YHWH's people will indeed have a home.

*Deuteronomy 6:10–13*

> When the LORD our God has brought you into the land that he swore to your ancestors, to Abraham, to Isaac, and to Jacob, to give you—a land with fine, large cities that you did not build, houses filled with all sorts of goods that you did not fill, hewn cisterns that you did not hew, vineyards and olive groves that you did not plant—and when you have eaten your fill, take care that you do not forget the LORD, who brought you out of the land of Egypt, out of the house of slavery. The LORD your God you shall fear; him you shall serve, and by his name alone you shall swear.

This old account of houses in ancient Israel acknowledges that houses are free, unearned, inexplicable gifts of grace. This uncommon conviction makes sense when we remember that the earliest theological vision and memory in Israel came out of marginal, disadvantaged peasants who were exploited and marginalized, without secure homes and endlessly in jeopardy.[4] Then there occurred a theological revolution as YHWH began to notice and to care and to move. Or as Gottwald prefers, this was a YHWH-authorized socio-political revolution whereby the citadels of monopoly were burned to the ground and goods were made available.[5] Peasants who dared never dream came into unexpected prosperity and security. The text calls this "the triumphs of the LORD, the triumphs of his peasantry in Israel" (Judg. 5:11). What could the peasants say except "Thanks," uttered with awe and gratitude. That is the beginning of a housing horizon in ancient Israel, houses "you did not fill," utter gift.

This newly given property is a covenantal arrangement. The ones who occupy the land and inhabit the houses are bound to the gracious giver: The LORD your God you shall fear, you shall serve, you shall swear by (Deut. 6:13). YHWH is now redefined by houses freely given, and houses are redefined by Yahwistic command. Houses are placed in the context of covenant, that is, of an alternative social vision and social requirement. The temptations are to have houses without YHWH, and YHWH without houses. But Deuteronomy will tolerate no retreat from covenantal definitions of social reality. Israel dare not forget, but must remember the strange gift of houses in a world where none seemed available. It is in the form of a house that this orphan people found mercy.

*Psalm 112*

> Praise the LORD!
> Happy are those who fear the LORD,
>     who greatly delight in his commandments.
> Their descendants will be mighty in the land;
>     the generation of the upright will be blessed.
> Wealth and riches are in their houses,
>     and their righteousness endures forever.
> They rise in the darkness as a light for the upright;
>     they are gracious, merciful, and righteous.
> It is well with those who deal generously and lend,
>     who conduct their affairs with justice.
> For the righteous will never be moved;
>     they will be remembered forever.
> They are not afraid of evil tidings;

their hearts are firm, secure in the LORD.
Their hearts are steady, they will not be afraid;
   in the end they will look in triumph on their foes.
They have distributed freely, they have given to the poor;
   their righteousness endures forever;
   their horn is exalted in honor.
The wicked see it and are angry;
   they gnash their teeth and melt away;
   the desire of the wicked comes to nothing.

Whereas Deuteronomy presents a tradition of unmerited gift (see also Deut. 7:7–8; 9:4–5), Psalm 112 offers a second opinion about how one comes to possess a house. This tradition sounds not like a community of peasants surprised at having a house, but rather like the voice of those well situated, who take their adequate housing and prosperity as their proper claim, achievement, and entitlement. Call it a tradition of "self-congratulatory righteousness."

Thus Psalm 112 describes those who fear God, keep commandments, and consequently are "mighty in the land." Their houses are filled with wealth and riches, and they are unendingly righteous. They practice justice and are "never moved," that is, never destabilized or placed in jeopardy. They are endlessly steady, secure, stable, generous, and the envy of the others. People who have secure houses find it persuasive to imagine the universe as stable, well-ordered, and moral, wherein good people are housed and others gnash their teeth and melt away. It is a simple interpretive maneuver to conclude that when people are reduced to poverty, they are the wicked, that is, the undeserving poor (see also Ps. 37:25–26).

Admittedly, I have cited an extreme case. But it is important because it helps form the limits of the difficult conversation in the Bible about housing. The two views in Deuteronomy and Psalms I have cited are sociologically conditioned, reflecting the experience of the *surprisingly* housed and the *complacently* housed. These two views run throughout Scripture and into our own time. When YHWH is social practice as well as sovereign Lord, it makes an enormous difference whether there are houses freely given out of God's abundant grace, or if houses are only a payout for a certain kind of socially approved conduct, that is, whether house is gift or payout.

*Deuteronomy 10:12–22*

I cite one other text that I would place at the point of origin in the biblical discussion of housing. This remarkable text voices at the same time the largest vision of YHWH's sovereignty and the most concrete ethical demand God can utter. On one hand, this is "God of gods, Lord of lords, . . . mighty and awesome" (Deut. 10:17). On the other hand, this is the God "who takes no bribe, who executes justice for the orphan and the widow, and who loves the strangers" (vv. 17–18). Indeed, this God is at work providing food and clothing for disenfranchised people (v. 18). This is doxological language, but even in doxological language it is clear that the Lord of lords and God of gods does not give food and clothing to vulnerable outsiders by supernaturalist fiat but by social practice.

Our point of interest in this text, however, is not in the indicative doxology, but in the derivative imperative:

> You shall also love the stranger,
> for you were strangers in the land of Egypt. (v. 19)

This is an extraordinary ethical imperative. First, the imperative asks Israel to do for others what has been done for it. You were displaced and were given a place. Now you give a place to the displaced. Second, and more powerfully, you do what God does. God loves the stranger . . . you love the stranger. God gives food and clothing . . . you give food and clothing. You be the social practice whereby God is made visible, available, and effective in the world. You be engaged in God's own work, as you yourself have experienced God's work, creating a safe place of dignity and wholeness for those without rights, claims, or leverage.

Even Psalm 112 does not fail to notice that the blessed housed still have their lives marked by generosity in society:

> They have distributed freely, they have given to the poor;
> their righteousness endures forever.
>
> Ps. 112:9

Thus the *tradition of revolutionary housing* and the *tradition of stable housing* both insist, with different voices, different passions, and different interests, that the housed must tend to the unhoused, because of history, memory, identity, and command. The hot tradition of covenant and the cool tradition of prudence converge. In both traditions, YHWH is a God who encompasses the life of Israel with a larger passion, a passion that works against one's immediate perceived vested interest for the sake of others.

These three texts form a baseline, a beginning point: House as *gift and promise* (Deut. 6:10–13), house as *reward for virtue* (Ps. 112), and house as *obligation to the stranger* (Deut. 10:12–22). All suggest a triangle: humanity, God, and house. House is given by God; house is definitionally for humanity.

## III

As you know, Israel remembers succumbing to a practice of greed that was systemic in character yet had concrete payouts in human misery and human rage. The disenfranchised in Israel were not regarded as "the unfortunate" or as the "less fortunate," as though social reality was a great mystery that happens without identifiable agent. Israel demystifies the process whereby poverty and homelessness are generated. The disenfranchised are seen to be victims of a rapacious economic system that had lost its rootage in exodus (by forgetting), in covenant (by not listening), and in wisdom (by being stupid). The following texts comment on the systemic act of forgetting, not listening, and being stupid as the way Israel tried to live its life, scuttling its identity founded in exodus, covenant, and wisdom. It is also clear, because of YHWH's governance, that such programmatic greed will lead to disaster.

Consider Isaiah 5:8–10:

> Ah, you who join house to house,
>   who add field to field,
> until there is room for no one but you,
>   and you are left to live alone
>   in the midst of the land!
> The LORD of hosts has sworn in my hearing:
> Surely many houses shall be desolate,
>   large and beautiful houses, without inhabitant.
> For ten acres of vineyard shall yield but one bath,
>   and a homer of seed shall yield a mere ephah.

D. N. Premnath has shown that this text reflects a process of latifundization, that is, of big owners buying up more and more land, necessarily displacing little owners, and forcing them to life without a place.[6] The poetry is poignant. "Until there is no one but you . . . you are left to live alone," because all the others have been driven out.[7]

Such economic rapaciousness evokes a solemn oath from the exodus God, who has ordered life differently. It is promised by God that the large houses will be abandoned, and the land will become utterly unproductive. The poet anticipates an enormous reversal of the economic process. No clue is given about how this will happen, because this is poetry and not social analysis. Whatever "secondary causes" there may be, we know the name of the primal cause of the destabilization that is sure to come with such neighbor abuse.

Amos 3:13–15 echoes this theme of reversal in housing:

> Hear, and testify against the house of Jacob,
>     says the Lord GOD, the God of hosts:
> On the day I punish Israel for its transgressions,
>     I will punish the altars of Bethel,
> and the horns of the altar shall be cut off
>     and fall to the ground.
> I will tear down the winter house as well as the summer house;
>     and the houses of ivory shall perish,
> and the great houses shall come to an end, says the LORD.

Again, the tone is a solemn oath on God's part to do the unthinkable against a society that has not thought before it acted. On one hand, the threat God speaks to an exploitative society is that the apparatus of religious legitimacy will be destroyed. In the horizon of Amos, the shrine at Bethel is the point for the bad-neighbor policies of the crown. On the other hand, the houses of the advantaged exploiters will be lost—winter houses, summer houses, houses of ivory, great houses. All will end because some have too many ill-gotten houses. It is telling that this poem is immediately followed in Amos 4:1–2 with a harsh indictment of excessive consumerism at the expense of the poor, which will end in exile. The critical poetry of the prophets is not so enthralled of present power arrangements that it cannot imagine what comes next. What comes next is derived from the God of the exodus, covenant, and wisdom who will not finally tolerate "excessive houses" at the expense of "no houses."

Biblical poetry attests that the status quo, when excessively brutalizing, cannot long be sustained. This prophetic analysis of the housed and the homeless anticipates that the first will be last, that the proud will be humbled, that as Hannah sings,

> Those who were full have hired themselves out for bread,
>    but those who were hungry are fat with spoil.
>
> 1 Sam. 2:5

And in the psalmic parallel to the Song of Hannah, the poem comes closer to our theme:

> He gives the barren woman a home,
>    making her the joyous mother of children.
>
> Ps. 113:9

The clearest expression of this anticipated inversion is in Micah 2:1–5 (briefly discussed in the previous chapter):

> Alas for those who devise wickedness
>    and evil deeds on their beds!
> When the morning dawns, they perform it,
>    because it is in their power.
> They covet fields, and seize them;
>    houses, and take them away;
> they oppress householder and house,
>    people and their inheritance.
> Therefore thus says the LORD:
> Now, I am devising against this family an evil
>    from which you cannot remove your necks;
> and you shall not walk haughtily,
>    for it will be an evil time.
> On that day they shall take up a taunt song against you,
>    and wail with bitter lamentation,
> and say, "We are utterly ruined;
>    [YHWH] alters the inheritance of my people;
> how he removes it from me!
>    Among our captors he parcels out our fields."
> Therefore you will have no one to cast the line by lot
>    in the assembly of the LORD.

The poem pictures the wicked who scheme in their beds. The poem reflects the peasant suspicion of anyone who stays too long in bed in the morning on the phone to the broker.[8] Before they even get up in the morning, they cut a deal, foreclose a mortgage, preempt a property. They covet fields, they take away houses. They violate the old promise of "houses you did not build." They play Monopoly and turn houses into hotels.

Well, says YHWH, they shall not "advance to go." They shall not collect $200. They shall go directly into social rejection. As they "devise" in verse 1, so now YHWH in verse 3 will "devise" against them. The tenth commandment, "You shall not covet," is a line drawn in the sand to protect the poor from the strong, who have such good brokers and smart lawyers. Coveting, even if it is legal, will finally bring terror of a very public kind. There will come evil, intrusion, and violation of those who mock the tenth commandment.

"On that day" of social payout, there will be grief, sad songs, despair, and funerals. "On that day," the monopolizers will notice that YHWH takes homes away from those who have seized too much. "On that day" an invading army will occupy the fields. The ones who have coveted will not be able to keep what they have taken.

While it may initially sound odd, the point of the final verse is ultimately clear. There will be an urgent meeting at the county court-house, that is, in "the assembly of the LORD," which will reorder the local economy. The purpose of the meeting is to draw new property lines, to redistribute the land. At that meeting, there will be no one to "cast the line" for you, no one to protect your interests, no one to advocate, no one to offer bids, no one to secure the land. When the land is redistributed, they will be left with nothing, displaced, with no place. They will be like the ones they victimized, and now they themselves will be utterly helpless.

This poem reflects village ethics, a small farmer-elder, railing against the urban economy, against the big banks and the cynical insurance companies, against an owned government and bought-off courts whose horizon does not extend past the class that owns them. The peasants are helpless against such great engines of wealth and power. This social analysis offered by Micah, however, is differ-ent, because YHWH is indeed a source of rescue, a line against self-sufficiency, a threat and advocate, a promiser.

These texts from Isaiah 5:8–10, Amos 3:13–15, and Micah 2:1–5, where social hurt and heavenly insistence converge, affirm that the power to produce homelessness will not go unchecked. There is an answering, and an inversion that the complacent cannot avoid.

## IV

As you know, the terrible inversion, anticipated by the prophets, happened in ancient Israel in 587, when Israel's rapacious socioeconomic policies terminated in deportation for some and devastation for all. In that terrible moment, responsible hope was required. Gone now are the harshest prophetic strictures; silenced is the relentless voice of threat.

I cite two texts from Third Isaiah, which show a community regrouping, to recover a human fabric destroyed by rapaciousness and displacement. The recovering of a viable human infrastructure requires concrete action by those who have not succumbed to selfishness. Instead of manipulative religious practice (Isa. 58:1–5), the rebuilding of the infrastructure that makes human life possible entails concrete neighbor-imperatives:

> Is not this the fast that I choose:
>     to loose the bonds of injustice,
>     to undo the thongs of the yoke,
> to let the oppressed go free,
>     and to break every yoke?
> Is it not to share your bread with the hungry,
>     and bring the homeless poor into your house;
> when you see the naked, to cover them,
>     and not to hide yourself from your own kin?
> Isa. 58:6–7

This must in the end be the primal text for our subject. In quick order, in five quick lines, we arrive at YHWH's central passion, Israel's central mandate, humanity's central hope. It is all "hands on." The metaphor concerns economics, as the ones who are characteristically in bonds and yokes and oppressed are of course the poor, locked in poverty cycles and inevitably lacking bread, housing, and clothing.

This great triad of neighborly love is at the same time the great triad of YHWH's passion for a reformed community of humanity in obedience.[9]

When this new fast of neighborly care is undertaken, light and healing come. The world works again, and God is again available and powerfully present (58:8–9a). The end result is the voice of YHWH assuring, "Here I am." I am here, where bread, and house, and clothing are shared. And where there is no such sharing, there will be no such healing presence.

This great imperative is matched seven chapters later by the most comprehensive promise in the Old Testament, a promise of new heaven, new earth, new city. That new city with a covenantal infrastructure is characterized by the poet in great detail. The detail concerns us:

> They shall build houses and inhabit them;
>     they shall plant vineyards and eat their fruit.
> They shall not build and another inhabit;
>     they shall not plant and another eat;
> for like the days of a tree shall the days of my people be,
>     and my chosen shall long enjoy the work of their hands.
>                                                   Isa. 65:21–22

The poem images a stable, equitable community in which threat, danger, greed, rapaciousness, instability, and displacement do not operate. The promise is that houses will be safe for living, not attacked, jeopardized, or foreclosed; that gardens will be safe and not usurped, invaded, occupied, or taxed to oblivion. The promise intends to override the danger of a disordered society, against which Amos had asserted:

> Therefore because you trample on the poor
>     and take from them levies of grain,
> you have built houses of hewn stone,
>     but you shall not live in them;
> you have planted pleasant vineyards,
>     but you shall not drink their wine.
>                                                   Amos 5:11

The terrible jeopardy voiced by Amos now is overridden in Isaiah 65. All is safe, "all is well and all shall be well."[10] This great promise is a word to keep us from succumbing to despair, even about the housing crisis. The command of Isaiah 58 makes clear that housing is indeed our work to do. It is to be done by caring, obedient people. That human work, however, is encompassed by the promise that God will create a new infrastructure of adequate, safe housing. It is promised we know not how. But it is promised that the present engines of homelessness will not prevail, that coveting cannot last, that monopoly and greed will not have a final say.

Thus the two texts from late Isaiah belong together. The *imperative* of chapter 58 counters our self-preoccupation. The *promise* of chapter 65 speaks against our exhausted despair. Our task is not a complete solution to the housing crisis, as though the imperative could manage without the promise. Our task, however, is ongoing and urgent, while God broods over ultimate possibility. It is clear in both texts, in both imperative and promise, against both selfishness and despair, that housing is a big deal to God. This God does not play monopoly for God's own aggrandizement, but intends for all to have houses, whether because the righteous deserve a house or because houses are freely given to all.

I conclude this section on a new infrastructure for exiles by reference to 1 Peter and the groundbreaking study of John Elliott.[11] In his book *A Home for the Homeless*, Elliott has seen that 1 Peter enjoins the Christian community to provide a home (*oikia*) for the homeless (*paroikia*), that is, for exiles and displaced persons. Further, Elliott has shown that the terms for "home and homeless" in the epistle have concrete socio-economic significance that should not be spiritualized. Elliott then suggests this epistle places the church under mandate to construct a new mediating structure for homefulness, larger than the family, smaller than the state, for those who had lost place in the homeless-inducing Roman Empire. Insofar as the epistle is linked to baptism—as it is, according to critical judgment—baptism becomes a gesture of embracing the work of *homefulness* in a world of *homelessness*.

## V

We have come a long way since Hosea 14:3, "In you the orphan finds mercy," but not that far, for I have argued that the entire life history of this community of faith is a struggle to be a home-making enterprise in a world endlessly productive of homelessness. As I have shaped our primal memory,

- The early season is marked by gift of homes you did not build, and by a demand to imitate God's home-making propensity.
- The middle season is dominated by greed, by the production of homelessness, and by the dire warnings of what happens to coveters.
- The late season of displacement issues in imperatives and promises that concern a new human, covenantal infrastructure.

What emerges from this study is that the eye of God and the hand of God's people are endlessly upon widows, orphans, and sojourners, those classic victims of displacement.[12] God intends that the displaced shall be commodiously placed in an ordered, secure human community. God has summoned and formed this Israel-church-new humanity in order to be a protector, an inventor, an alternative, a gadfly, a subverter, a hope, that the dominant modes of exile-production need not prevail in the world.

It is stunning that the vision of the church among exiles in 1 Peter reclaims the identity of the liberated slaves who rushed to Sinai to rethink and repractice a covenantal human infrastructure. It is from Exodus, Sinai, and Moses that Peter writes:

But you are a chosen race, a royal priesthood, a holy nation, God's own people, in order that you may proclaim the mighty acts of him who called you out of darkness into his marvelous light.

Once you were not a people,
    but now you are God's people;
once you had not received mercy,
    but now you have received mercy.
                1 Pet. 2:9–10

The church is invited to see itself set in the world with a priestly role, to proclaim and practice God's mighty acts, to be the *mode of mercy* that orphans receive from God. The church has the chance to let the practice of mercy touch the reality of God's displaced orphans.

I conclude with four questions that may haunt us as we strive to do this awesome work:

1. Is it true that some lack a home because some have too much house?
2. Is it true that we seek too much house at the expense of our neighbors, because we ourselves are deeply homeless?[13]
3. Is it true that one cannot care deeply about homes for others, until we find our true homefulness?
4. "Therefore do not worry, saying, 'What shall we eat?' or 'What shall we drink?' or 'What will we wear?' For it is the Gentiles who strive for all these things; and indeed your heavenly Father knows that you need all these things" (Matt. 6:31–32). What did Jesus mean when he said this?

We are, as you know, children of the Holy One, who already knows we need all these things—as do the others.

## Questions for Reflection

1. With the housing crisis in mind, where do you see Hosea's words, "In you the orphan finds mercy" (Hos. 14:3), as a need or a reality today?

2. Which model or models resonate most with you: house as *gift and promise*, house as *reward for virtue*, or house as *obligation to the stranger*? In contrast, what models seem most prevalent as a social practice or political viewpoint in today's society?

3. What does economic rapaciousness look like in your community?

4. How do you understand the imperative of Isaiah 58 and the promise of Isaiah 65 as the church's task now?

Chapter 5

# Cadences That Redescribe

## Speech among Exiles

$G$od's gracious acts in the Bible tend to fall on and be requested by people in need. The prevailing circumstance in the Bible that left Israel in acute need of God's gracious deliverance was exile. Exile, that is, social, cultural displacement, is not primarily geographical, but it is liturgical and symbolic.[1] This was the case with the Jews in exile in the sixth century BCE, as it is in our Western culture presently. In defining exile, Alan Mintz writes: "The catastrophic element in events [of exile] is defined as the power to shatter the existing paradigms of meaning, especially as regards the bonds between God and the people of Israel."[2] In such a situation, where "paradigms of meaning" are shattered, exiles must pay careful and sustained attention to speech, because it requires inordinately disciplined and imaginative speech to move through the shattering to newly voiced meaning. Mintz suggests that in exile, the primal speakers (poets) attempt "first to *represent the catastrophe* and then to *reconstruct, replace, or redraw the threatened paradigm of meaning*, and thereby make creative survival possible."[3]

I find Paul Ricoeur's phrasing a useful way to understand what is required and what is possible for speech in such situations. Ricoeur speaks about "limit experiences" that permit and require "limit expressions."[4] Limit experiences are those in which all conventional descriptions and explanations are inadequate. When one is pushed experientially to such extremity, one cannot continue to mouth commonplaces but must instead utter something "odd."[5] The odd expression must effectively *redescribe* reality away from and apart from all

73

usual assumptions.[6] Such speech invites the speaker and the listener into a world that neither has known before this utterance.

It is clear that in exile something utterly new has to be uttered in daring speech that evokes newness by deploying in fresh ways speech that is already known and trusted. In order to serve as "redescription," the already trusted speech must be uttered in daring, venturesome ways that intensify, subvert, and amaze.

By utilizing the theme of exile as an analogue by which to describe our current social situation in the West, I suggest that our loss of the white, male, Western, colonial hegemony, which is deeply displacing for some, is indeed a limit experience, whereby we are pushed to the edge of our explanatory and coping powers. Such experience requires limit expression. Such a consideration is applicable to preachers, precisely because preachers in such a limit experience have obligation and possibility of being the very ones who can give utterance both to "represent the catastrophe" and to "reconstruct, replace, or redraw" the paradigms of meaning that will permit "creative survival." I suggest that the preaching task now is nothing less than that twofold task.

In what follows I will consider four examples of limit expression that were utilized in that ancient exile of sixth-century Judeans, in order that their limit experience of displacement could be embraced and moved through. My thought is that there are clues here for our own speech practice in a time of acute displacement and bewilderment.

## I. Lamentation and Complaint

The first task among exiles is to represent the catastrophe, to state what is happening by way of loss in vivid images so that the loss can be named by its right name and publicly faced in the depth of its negativity. Such naming and facing permits the loss to be addressed to God, who is implicated as less than faithful in a context of fickleness and failure. Such speech requires enough candor to dare to utter the torrent of sensitivities that cluster, such as pain, loss, grief, shame, and rage. For this naming and facing, this ancient Jewish community found its best speech by appeal to the liturgical tradition of *lamentation* (expressing sadness) and *complaint* (expressing indignation).[7]

The richest, most extreme statement of sadness, punctuated by loss, helplessness, and vulnerability, is the book of Lamentations.[8] It is not much studied or used among us, no doubt because it has seemed so remote from our cultural situation. If, however, we are now in a new situation of profound loss, as I have suggested, this poetry could be for us an important "speech resource." The little book of Lamentations consists of five extended poems of grief over the destruction of Jerusalem (which I have suggested as an analogue to the loss of our accustomed privilege and certitude). In the first poem (chapter 1), the bereft city of Jerusalem is "like a widow," abandoned, shamed, vulnerable, subject to abuse, without an advocate or defender (Lam. 1:1). The recurring theme of the abandonment of Jerusalem is expressed as "no one to comfort her" (1:2, 9, 16, 17); "no resting place" (v. 3); "no pasture" (v. 6); "no one to help" (v. 7). The imagery is of a woman overwhelmed with tears, under assault, and subject to abuse.[9] While there is in 3:21–33 a powerful statement of hope and confidence, the collection of Lamentations ends with a sense of "forsakenness":

> Why have you forgotten us completely?
> Why have you forsaken us these many days?
> Lam. 5:20

This same sense of being "forgotten" is evident in the more abrasive and indignant complaint of Psalm 74. Here the poet is more aggressive in describing to God the situation of dismay and in pressing God to act.[10] The poem provides for God a play-by-play of what "your foes" have done to "your holy place" (Ps. 74:4, see vv. 4–9). It then moves to a doxology (see below), recalling to God God's own powerful miracles of the past (vv. 12–17). These concern God's sovereign rule over all of creation, and God's capacity to bring life out of chaos. By juxtaposing the present calamity of the temple and God's glorious past, the poem makes intercession that God should now act, both to defeat the impious enemies and to act so that "the downtrodden" are not "put to shame" (74:21, see vv. 18–23). One is struck in this psalm with the directness of speech, the candor about the current trouble, which is catastrophic, and the vigor with which God is expected to act in gracious fidelity.

Through both the lamentation and the psalm of complaint, the catastrophic is vividly represented, to make it as palpable to God as it is to the community. My suggestion, insofar as our current Western dismay is a parallel to this ancient travesty, is that a primary pastoral task is to voice the felt loss, indignation, and bewilderment that are among us. The reason extreme imagery is required is that the speech must cut through the enormous self-deception of political/economic euphemism. For the truth is that the old, settled advantage in the world upon which we have counted is as over and gone as was Jerusalem's temple. Sadness, pain, and indignation are not inappropriate responses to the loss, either then or now. They require abrasive, insistent speech to be available, and ancient Israel gives us a script for our own daring representation of the trouble.

## II. Assurance

In the laments and complaints, Israel speaks to God. Israel takes the initiative in rightly naming its displacement to God. In times of debilitating dismay, it is the one who experiences the dismay who must courageously come to speech.[11] This is abundantly clear in the speech of ancient Israel. But Israel's limit expressions are not restricted to the voice of Israel. The voice of YHWH also sounds in the daring rhetoric of the exile, precisely in the context where Israel had sensed its abandonment by God. Indeed, in the poetry of Second Isaiah, God acknowledges that God has been silent too long and will now break that silence in powerful speech. God says,

> For a long time I have held my peace,
>   I have kept still and restrained myself;
> now I will cry out like a woman in labor,
>   I will gasp and pant.
> Isa. 42:14; cf. 62:1

In the "salvation oracles" of Second Isaiah, Israel hears the classic assurance that God is present with and for Israel, even in its dismay and displacement. Most precisely and succinctly, this oracle of assurance asserts on God's lips, "Fear not, for I am with you" (see Isa. 41:13, 14; 43:1–5; 44:8; Jer. 30:10–11).[12] Joseph Sittler among others has seen that this speech is closely paralleled to the way a parent reassures a child who has had a nightmare.[13] Such parental assurance is indeed a redescription. This assurance is nightmare-ending speech, for it asserts a caring presence that is trusted enough and powerful enough to override the sense of absence evoked by the exile. Now, in this utterance, what had seemed to be a place of absence is known to be a place of presence, thereby invested with great potential for life.

What counts for our consideration is the situation-transforming capacity of the utterance, what Ricoeur would term "redescription." Thus Lamentations 5:20 ends with haunting sense of being "forgotten" and "forsaken":

> Why have you *forgotten* us completely?
> Why have you *forsaken* us these many days?

In Isaiah 49:14, the same two terms are reiterated, probably deliberately quoted:

> But Zion said, "The LORD *has forsaken* me,
> my Lord *has forgotten* me."

But then in Isaiah 49:15–16, these haunting fearful questions are answered by the God who does not forget or abandon:

> Can a woman *forget* her nursing child,
> or show no compassion for the child of her womb?
> Even these may *forget*,
> yet I will not *forget* you.
> See, I have inscribed you on the palms of my hands;
> your walls are continually before me.

Or in Isaiah 54:10, after conceding that there had been a brief abandonment of Israel by God (vv. 7–8), and after comparing the devastation of the exile to the flood in Genesis (v. 9), the poet has God utter a sweeping assurance of God's reliable durability:[14]

> For the mountains may depart
> and the hills be removed,
> but my *steadfast love* shall not depart from you,
> and my *covenant of peace* shall not be removed,
> says the LORD, who has *compassion* on you.
> v. 10

This triad of YHWH's gracious characteristics—steadfast love, covenant of peace, compassion—is more than enough to override the flood, to overcome the absence and shame, and to overmatch the terror of exile.

We are so familiar with such assurances that we may fail to notice what a daring act of faith such an utterance is, how blatantly it speaks against and beyond perceived circumstance, in order to "reconstruct, replace, or redraw the threatened paradigm of meaning." It is an act of powerful faith on the part of the speaker, but also on the part of the listener. The intent of the assurance is to create faith in the listener. The exile was widely seen to be a season of God's absence, and now this poet dares to assert that God is present in that very circumstance, graciously at work to bring a newness out of the defeat.

The analogue in our own time is for the preacher-poet of the gospel to make such an utterance in the midst of our failed privilege and hegemony. The utterance of assurance is not to prop up the old paradigm, for the assurance comes only after the "representation of the catastrophe," that is, after the felt and expressed situation of lamentation and complaint. The assurance asserts that in the very midst of *economic displacement* and *bewilderment about sexuality*, where all old certitudes are in profound jeopardy, just these meanings of a new kind are being wrought by the power and fidelity of God, "new things" shaped like covenantal faithfulness that will become visible only in, with, and through the displacement.[15] Such utterances are indeed "by faith alone." But then, that is always how the gospel is uttered in such problematic circumstance.

## III. Doxologies of Defiance

The counterpole to lamentation and complaint is the hymn of praise that emerges from "victory songs." Hymns are sung when situations of great trouble are transformed by the gracious power of God. Israel has been singing such songs since the deliverance from Egypt (Exod. 15:1–18, 21). These daring doxologies sing what Israel has seen and heard about the decisive power and reliable commitment of YHWH to intrude in life-giving ways in circumstances of defeat, disorder, and death. Thus the doxology of remembrance in Psalm 74:12–17 reaches all the way back to creation and to God's capacity to order chaos. And the despondent worshiper in Psalm 77:11–20 ponders the remembered exodus. Out of these treasured, concrete memories, Israel's hymns also constitute acts of hope, confident that what God has done in the past is what God will do in the present and in the future. In the exile, the doxologies are not primarily acts of remembering God's past "wonders," but they are anticipatory assertions concerning what God is about to do. Israel is summoned to sing a "new song," to sing praise for God's sovereign liberating action that is now about to occur (Isa. 42:10).

In exile, it was "self-evident" that the Babylonian gods had triumphed, that YHWH had failed, either because of weakness or because of indifference. Either way, the evidence suggested that loyalty to YHWH no longer worked or was no longer worth practicing, because other powers could give more reliable and immediate payoffs. The poetry of Second Isaiah, however, will not accept that "self-evident" reading of reality. The hymns are assertions against the evidence, insisting that YHWH's saving power is at the break of new activity. Israel had concluded that God does not care:

> Why do you say, O Jacob,
>   and speak, O Israel,
> "My way is hidden from the LORD,
>   and my right is disregarded by my God"?
>                                           Isa. 40:27

The responding hymn of verses 28–31 asserts in wondrous lyric that YHWH is the God of all generations, past, present, future, is not weary or faint or powerless, but gives power to those who hope. The outcome is not only a statement about God, but an assurance to those who trust this God:

> [T]hose who wait for the LORD shall renew their strength,
>   they shall mount up with wings like eagles,
> they shall run and not be weary,
>   they shall walk and not faint.
>                                           v. 31

Notice that the doxology completely rejects the notion of the rule of the Babylonian gods. Against their apparent rule, it is, so the hymn asserts, in fact YHWH who holds power and who gives power (cf. Isa. 46:1–4).

That same contrast is evident in the defiant doxology of Isaiah 41:21–29. Negatively the gods of Babylon are called to give account of themselves, and they fail miserably (vv. 21–23). This leads to the conclusion that they are nothing, nothing at all. Moreover, those who trust such "nothing gods" are as "nothing" as their gods.

> You, indeed, are nothing
>    and your work is nothing at all;
>    whoever chooses you is an abomination.
> Isa. 41:24

Positively, it is YHWH who is able to act visibly, decisively, and transformatively (vv. 25–27). Israel's doxologies are characteristically against the data, inviting Israel to live in a "redescribed world," in which meaning has been "reconstructed, replaced, or redrawn."

In our own situation, the hymnic act of praise has become largely innocuous. It happens often among us that praise is either escapist fantasy, or it is a bland affirmation of the status quo. In fact, doxology is a daring political, polemical act that serves to dismiss certain loyalties and to embrace and legitimate other loyalties and other shapes of reality.[16]

In Second Isaiah, the hymnic wager is on YHWH's intention for homecoming, and therefore on the refusal of the Babylonian gods, who seek to define the world in noncovenantal ways. In our situation of upheaval and confusion, hymns that celebrate the God of the Bible wager on a covenantal-neighborly world powered by the neighborliness of God, and wager against any characterization of the world that bets on selfishness, greed, fear, abuse, or despair. Our current world of bewilderment is often described as though everything good is ending, as though the forces of chaos have won. This hymnic tradition authorizes the church to identify and redescribe this present place as the arena in which the rule of the creator-liberator God is working a wondrous newness. Our singing and utterance of such lyric faith assert that we will not submit to the gods of fear and anticovenantal power relations. In such a situation as ours, the words and music for a "new song" are acts of powerful renewal.

## IV. Promises

The assurances and hymns upon which we have commented are anticipatory. They look to the resolve of YHWH to work a newness that is not yet visible or in hand. In oracles of promise, however, exiles have a way of speech that is more directly and singularly preoccupied with God's sure future. Israel believes that God can indeed work a newness out of present shambles and that that newness will more fully embody God's goodwill for the world. It is cause for amazement that Israel's most daring and definitional promises were uttered in exile, that is, precisely when the evidence seemed to preclude such hope. The promises are assertions that God is not a prisoner of circumstance but that God can call into existence that which does not exist (cf. Rom. 4:17).

Here are three of the best known and most powerful of such exilic promises. In Jeremiah 31:31–34, the promise asserts that God will work a new covenant with Israel that is aimed at Torah obedience (v. 33) but is rooted in the overriding reality of forgiveness (v. 34).[17] The dominant assumption about exile in the Old Testament, propounded especially in the Deuteronomic tradition, is that exile is punishment (2 Kgs. 17:7–23; see even Isa. 40:2). This promise, in the face of a theology of guilt-and-punishment, is an assertion that forgiveness will overpower sin, and Israel's primal theological reality is the future-creating graciousness of YHWH, who will "remember their sin no more."[18]

In Ezekiel 37:1–14, the prophet Ezekiel searches for an adequate metaphor for exile and homecoming. The most extreme imagery available is that exile equals death. From death, there is no hope, for the power of death is strong and decisive. In a radical, rhetorical break, however, the prophet dares to assert that by the power of God's spirit, "I am going to open your graves," that is, "I will place you on your own soil" (vv. 12–14). Exile is not the last word; death is not the last reality. Israel's situation is not hopeless, because God's transformative wind (spirit) blows even in the dismay of exile, in order to work a newness toward life.

The poem of Isaiah 65:17–25 (which may be dated slightly after the return from exile in 520 BCE) offers a "portrayal of salvation" in stunning anticipatory fashion. The poet anticipates a new earth and a new Jerusalem characterized by new social relations, new economic possibilities, and new communion with God. Indeed, the poet foresees a complete and concrete inversion of Israel's current situation of hopelessness.

Notice that all of the promises, specific as they are, are cast as God's own speech, the authority for which is found not in any visible circumstance, but in the trustworthiness of the God who speaks. It is God's own resolve to work a newness that will impinge upon what seems to be a closed, hopeless situation. Exiles inevitably must reflect upon the power of promise, upon the capacity of God to work a newness against all circumstance.[19]

Promise has become nearly an alien category among us. That is partly an intellectual problem for us, because our Enlightenment perception of reality does not believe that there can be any newness "from the outside" that can enter our fixed world. The loss of promise is also a function of our privilege in the world, whereby we do not in fact want newness, but only an enhancement and guarantee of our preferred present tense.

As white, male, Western privilege comes to an end, some are likely to experience that "ending" as terrible loss, which evokes fear and resentment.[20] Evangelical faith, however, dares to identify what is (for some) an alienating circumstance as the matrix for God's newness (for all). Thus evangelical speech functions to locate the hunches, hints, and promises that seem impossible to us that God will indeed work in the midst of our frightening bewilderment. However, the preacher will work primarily not from visible hints and hunches, precisely because hope is "the conviction of things not seen," a conviction rooted in the trusted character of God.

## V. The Ministry of Language

Speech, or as Mintz terms it, "the ministry of language," is one of the few available resources for exile.[21] Exiles are characteristically stripped of all else except speech. What exiles do is to speak their "mother tongue," that is, the speech learned as children from mother, as a way to maintain identity in a situation that is identity-denying. In that ancient world of displacement, the Judeans treasured speech that was "redescriptive," precisely because it was not derived from or sanctioned by the managers of the exile. It was, rather, derived from older speech practice of the covenanted community and sanctioned by the evangelical chutzpah of poets who dared to credit such defiant utterances as complaints, lamentations, assurances, hymns, and promises. These are indeed forms of speech from Israel's "mother tongue."

In the "modernist" church of our time (liberal and conservative), there has been a loss of "mother-speech," partly because of subtle epistemological erosion, and partly because we imagine that other forms of speech are more credible and "make more sense." The truth is, however, that speech other than our own gradually results in the muteness of the church, for we have nothing left to say when we have no way left to say it. Exiles need, first of all and most of all, a place in which to practice liberated speech that does not want or receive the legitimacy of context. I take it that the old "paradigms of meaning" are indeed deeply under threat among us. We can scarcely pretend otherwise. We may learn from our ancestors in faith that in such a context, we must indeed "represent the catastrophe" and then "reconstruct, replace, or redraw" the paradigms of meaning. Both tasks are demanding. It belongs nonetheless to the speakers rooted in this tradition of liberated, defiant, anticipatory speech to take up these tasks. It is in, with, and from such speech that there comes, gracefully, "all things new."

## Questions for Reflection

1. When have you participated, as a speaker or a listener, in speech that tries to capture a new reality or aims to describe a "limit experience"?

2. What biblical stories or texts are your speech resources, providing a script that captures—or even transforms and redescribes—your life experiences?

3. What hymns or doxological verses of praise remind you of the promise of God to bring newness in the midst of bewilderment or exile?

4. How does your faith community function as a place for exiles to practice liberated speech?

# PART TWO

# Practices of Biblical Grace

Chapter 6

# Sabbath as Alternative

*I*t is a great misfortune that in our United States Puritan legacy, the Sabbath is perceived as a restrictive, killjoy practice to be overcome in emancipated self-actualization. To the contrary, in ancient Israel the Sabbath is a mighty practice that sustains a peculiar faith identity in a political economy that seeks eagerly to overcome that peculiar identity, which is seen as a hindrance to larger economic effectiveness. That peculiar faith identity, moreover, has immense significance for the healthy ordering of the political economy.

## I. Looking Both Ways

The Sabbath commandment stands at the center of the Decalogue, the first injunctions that characterize the covenant made at Sinai (Exod. 20:1–17).[1] The Sabbath commandment occupies considerable textual space (vv. 8–11). Patrick Miller has shown that this critical position in the Ten Commandments means that this Sabbath commandment looks both ways.[2] It looks back to commandments one to three, which concern God; this backward look suggests that the God who gives the commandments practices Sabbath and is a God of rest, not a God of endless restless anxious production. But the Sabbath commandment also looks forward to commandments five to ten, which concern neighborly relations. This means that respectful neighborly relations are premised on restfulness, so that such relations are not driven by anxious, aggressive, self-protective conduct and policy. The Sabbath commandment looks both ways

87

and provides for a restfulness for both God and neighbor. It is possible to think that such a commandment eventuates in the two great commandments to "love God and neighbor" (Mark 12:28–34), to respect the restfulness of both parties: don't crowd, don't demand, don't coerce.

## II. The Gift of Being Re-*nepheshed*

The Sabbath commandment, like all these commandments, sits in a thick interpretive tradition. Interpretation is required in order to probe what the commandment might mean in actual practice in various particular circumstances. Indeed, there are two quite different normative interpretations of the Sabbath commandment. The more familiar one is in the Sinai event of Exodus 20, where the ground for Sabbath rest is creation:

> For in six days the LORD made heaven and earth, the sea, and all that is in them, but rested the seventh day; therefore the LORD blessed the sabbath day and consecrated it. (Exod. 20:11)

This grounding of Sabbath appeals to the rhythm of creation in a seven-day routine that is performed and acknowledged in the creation narrative (Gen. 1:1–2:4a). In that narrative, God rested on the Sabbath day after six days of work (Gen. 2:3). God is not endlessly at work, not endlessly anxious about the world as creation, not endlessly engaged in its generation or maintenance. God exhibits confidence that the world, infused with God's blessing, has a sustaining capacity of its own.

Perhaps the most interesting and important biblical exposition of this claim is voiced in the more tedious and unfamiliar provision for the tabernacle in Exodus 25–31. In that long instruction, God details to Moses the tabernacle as an apparatus for divine presence, culminating in the coming of God's glory into the tabernacle (Exod. 40:34–38). The instruction is given in seven divine speeches, each introduced with the formula "The LORD said [or spoke] to Moses" (Exod. 25:1; 30:11, 17, 22, 34; 31:1, 12).[3] Many interpreters conclude that these seven speeches are designed to match the seven days of creation in Genesis 1–2.[4] Moses is instructed to make a liturgical world that articulates creation as it should be, so that Israel, in its worship, may for a time move from the conflicted, dangerous world of its circumstance to the rightly ordered world of creation as offered in liturgy. In that sequence of seven divine speeches, the first six concern liturgical furniture and equipment, and provision for proper priestly procedure and decorum. It is something of a surprise that the seventh speech, not unlike the seventh day of creation, is very different and concerns exactly the observance of Sabbath. The rightly ordered world of worship culminates in Sabbath observance (Exod. 31:12–17).

These verses insist upon the Sabbath with intense urgency, as a "sign forever" of a perpetual covenant between YHWH and Israel. No other provision in these speeches has that claim attached to it. The rhetoric suggests a binding of the two partners not unlike the commandments in Exodus 20, wherein commandments one to three concerning God and commandments five to ten concerning neighbor are bound together in the fourth commandment.

Notice should especially be taken of the final clause of Exodus 31:17, which concludes the seven speeches of instruction to Moses. It is said that God rested on the seventh day. Our usual translation is that God "was refreshed." Sabbath is for refreshment! Even God requires such refreshment! But the term rendered in this way is a verbal form of the noun *nephesh*, which we usually render as "life, self, soul." The nominal form occurs many times, but the verbal form, as here, occurs only three times in the Hebrew Bible. In Exodus 23:12, it is used in a way parallel to 31:17, which concerns Sabbath rest: ". . . so that your homeborn slave and the resident alien may be refreshed." The other use is in 2 Samuel 16:14. David, fleeing for his life along with his faithful entourage, arrives at the Jordan River and "there he refreshed himself." Each use concerns refreshment, given in the form of rest or enlivening water—but "refreshed" fails to convey the meaning of the noun that we translate as "self, soul, life." As suggested above in chapter 2, a stronger translation would be that God, in Exodus 31:17, was re-*nepheshed*, that is, received back "self, life, soul" that had been depleted or diminished by the work of creation. Such a translation indicates the urgency of Sabbath, because the usage recognizes that one's life (*nephesh*)—even God's life (God's *nephesh*)—can be depleted or diminished, and must be restored by proper Sabbath keeping.

Such a translation makes clear that in Exodus 20:8–11, Genesis 2:3, and Exodus 31:17 Sabbath keeping is no mere incidental practice. It is rather an acknowledgment of the human condition and of God's provision for human frailty and fragility, made clear in the affirmation that even God's own life or self can be depleted and diminished. Thus, Sabbath is a mighty antidote to an economy of depletion and diminishment, because it entails participation in a community that does not believe that human well-being and worth are established by endless productivity. The commandment is thus an act of resistance against such an economy. It is also provision for an alternative way. That alternative in Genesis 1–2 relies on the fruitful blessing of the earth. In Exodus 31 it is reliance on the presence of God as life-giver, assured in the apparatus of the liturgy.

Sabbath, then, is not just a practice. It is a life choice to belong to a different humanity. Michael Fishbane sees that Sabbath is an act of divestment from productivity of the world, a divestment that knows that life is a gift, not an accomplishment or a possession:

> A sense of inaction takes over, and the day does not merely mark the stoppage of work or celebrate the completion of creation, but enforces the value that the earth is a gift of divine creativity, given to mankind in sacred trust. On the Sabbath, the practical benefits of technology are laid aside, and one tries to stand in the cycle of natural time, without manipulation or interference. To the degree possible, one must also attempt to bring the qualities of inaction and rest into the heart and mind.[5]

The matter of Sabbath keeping as life choice for an alternative existence is echoed in the poetry of Isaiah 56 concerning participation in the postexilic community of Judaism. The prophetic poem makes provision for the inclusion in the community of "foreigners and eunuchs," two groups that some wanted to exclude. Most remarkably, their inclusion is premised generally on keeping covenant, but specifically on keeping Sabbath:

> To the eunuchs who keep my sabbaths,
>     who choose the things that please me
>     and hold fast my covenant . . .
> all who keep the sabbath, and do not profane it,

and hold fast my covenant—
these I will bring to my holy mountain.

                                    Isa. 56:4, 6–7

It is noteworthy that Sabbath keeping is the only specific requirement, which suggests that it is this disciplined act that most distinguishes the community of covenant from the dominant economy of that time. The culminating invitation of inclusiveness is in the wake of Sabbath keeping:

> [T]hese [foreigners and eunuchs] I will bring to my holy mountain,
>     and make them joyful in my house of prayer . . .
> for my house shall be called a house of prayer
>     for all peoples.

                                         v. 7

One might judge that in a Sabbath-less society not all would be welcome at worship, because in a production-propelled society, social rank, social power, and social access are sure to be hierarchal, based on worth established by endless productivity. Sabbath is a great equalizer: all are welcome, because their worth is not based on productivity, a criterion that foreigners and eunuchs perhaps could not meet.

## III. Sabbath as Emancipation

The Sabbath commandment is decisively altered in Deuteronomy; this is the only substantive change in this section of the Decalogue (Deut. 5:12–15). Here the commandment on Sabbath is no longer grounded in God's rest at creation, but rather in the exodus event, which was an emancipation from the exploitative labor practices of Pharaoh in Egypt, as we saw in chapter 1 above. The exodus was a decisive disruption of Pharaoh's production schedule, which imposed coercive pressure on the bodies of bondaged workers. The exodus is narrated as a one-time event. But the Sabbath is a way of assuring that the memory of the exodus has continuing contemporary force for emancipatory significance. It is to be noted that in Deuteronomy 5:14, on the Sabbath day, working animals, slaves, and immigrants (those without assured rights) are all "as well as you," that is, *all* entitled to rest. The Sabbath is a day of social equalization for those who on all other days are quite unequal.

In the tradition of Deuteronomy, the Sabbath commandment provides the basis for an extended series of economic provisions that are designed to protect the weak from predation.[6] The series includes:

- restrictions on charging interest on loans (23:19–20)
- limitation on loan collateral concerning the poor (24:10–13, 17–18)
- prohibition of "wage theft" by withholding payment to laborers (24:14–15)
- provision for the widow, orphan, and immigrant (the most economically vulnerable groups in that ancient economy) by leaving agricultural produce after harvest, thus anticipating the pernicious "laws of enclosure" enacted in modern time (24:19–22)
- limitation of physical punishment in order to maintain human dignity for the guilty (25:1–3)
- requirement of honest weights and measures in commerce (25:13–16)

All these provisions are intended to prevent predatory practices against the vulnerable. Twice the motivation for the commandment is remembrance of the exodus (24:18, 22).

Moreover, the tradition of Deuteronomy provides the basis for much of the prophetic critique of a predatory economy. Deuteronomy is the lead tradition that defines social relationships in terms of covenant that regards all the members of the community as neighbors. Thus, the economy is to be a neighborly practice that curbs excessive greed and exploitation in the interest of sustaining social relationships of dignity, respect, and security.

One prophetic articulation concerning Sabbath that lives in the same world as Deuteronomy is the oracle of Amos 8:4–8. The prophet addresses those who exploit the poor by using dishonest weights, who reduce the poor to tradable commodities. In the oracle, God vows disruptive action against the "pride of Jacob," unspecified actions that will cause the land to tremble, that will bring mourning and chaos like an overflowing Nile River. The image is of an exploitative economy that victimizes those without resources. What interests us is that such merchants and traders resent Sabbath, which inconveniently interrupts their commercial dealings. They are eager that Sabbath should end in order to resume their predatory practices. They rightly recognize that the Sabbath is intended precisely to disrupt such practices, to give the vulnerable a respite from exploitation. In the horizon of Deuteronomy, Sabbath is not only provision for a day of rest. It is in fact a taproot for a political economy that is imagined and practiced differently, because in it economic concerns are subordinated to and governed by neighborly relationships. The economy does not function autonomously but is designed to serve the common good of the neighborhood.

## IV. A Paradigmatic Shift

The preamble to the Decalogue indicates that the Ten Commandments are designed as an alternative and counter to the regime of Pharaoh:

> I am the LORD your God, who brought you out of the land of Egypt, out of the house of slavery. (Exod. 20:2)

It turns out that the narrative of exodus emancipation is not an isolated event of ancient memory. It is in fact programmatic and paradigmatic for all that follows in Israel. Thus, we may make a case that the entire Decalogue is designed to fend off the pressures and dangers and seductions of all Pharaonic economies.[7] As we saw in chapter 1, Pharaoh's socioeconomic practice is intense, and intensified in the series of imperatives issued by Pharaoh to his supervisors and taskmasters, requiring that the Hebrew slaves be more and more productive of larger brick quotas, even in circumstances that hinder their productivity (Exod. 5:4–19). Behind this inflammatory picture of exploitation there is the more sober narrative report of Genesis 47:13–25, which probes how Pharaoh's economic policies worked. It is clear that Pharaoh is an accumulator of land and food, propelled by his double nightmare of scarcity (see Gen. 41:1–7). His policy grew out of his fear! Joseph, an erstwhile Hebrew, is Pharaoh's willing agent who works against his own Hebrew people. Amid the scarcity resulting from famine, Joseph, on behalf of Pharaoh, systematically takes money from the hapless peasants. Then he takes their cattle, their means of production.[8] Finally Joseph takes their land and their bodies into slavery. The narrative reports in summary:

> All the Egyptians sold their fields, because the famine was severe upon them; and the land became Pharaoh's. (Gen. 47:20)

Pharaoh's land seizure is reported as a sustained strategy for reducing subsistence farmers to slavery, thus assuring that Pharaoh would have an endless, reliable supply of cheap labor among those who had no economic leverage whereby to resist. Pharaoh's strategy is to render people vulnerable to a kind of dependence that is sustained by impossible debt. In his world, everything and everyone are reduced to a tradable commodity; laborers are situated so as to be unable to assert any agency in their own history.

It follows, of course, that in Pharaoh's regime there was no Sabbath rest for anyone. Certainly not for the slaves or for the work animals, and likely not for the taskmasters and supervisors, and surely not for Pharaoh himself. All social relationships in a society without Sabbath rest are reduced to commodity transactions, reinforced by fear, the threat of violence, and, when necessary, real violence (see Exod. 1:13–14).

In that world the exodus could be readily remembered through bodily suffering. The Sinai commands are an effort by YHWH, the God of liberation, to counter Pharaoh's policies of coercive commoditization. By keeping Sabbath, Israel practically and bodily imagines a political economy that is not reduced to commodity transactions, an economy wherein even the vulnerable are respected and treated as neighbors who are entitled to security.

The Sabbath tradition in ancient Israel, along with the exodus narrative, was an articulation of reality that could be reenacted and reperformed in many new circumstances. Thus, in usurpative Jerusalem (and especially in the usurpative reign of Solomon with his forced labor and tax-collecting prowess), Sabbath issues a mighty protest and alternative. Thus, Sabbath practice is life beyond the reach of the predatory practice of Pharaoh, often belatedly reperformed by those who imitate Pharaoh. We cannot fully understand the Sabbath command, in ancient or contemporary setting, unless we are vigorously alert to the Pharaonic capacity that is endlessly reperformed in economies that are propelled by the logic of scarcity.

## V. The Sabbatical Principle

Patrick Miller has shrewdly seen that the Sabbath commandment issues in a "sabbatical principle" whereby the entire practice of political economy is redefined by Sabbath claims.[9] The "sabbatical principle" shows up in two major Torah provisions, which evidently derive from Sabbath, as they also are according to a regime of "sevens."

In Deuteronomy 15:1–18, a pivotal text for the tradition of Deuteronomy, the "year of release" provides that every seven years there is to be a remission of debts. This commandment clearly intends to subordinate the economy to the enhancement of neighborly social relations, so that neighbors count for more than either debts or wealth. Special attention is given to the needy (v. 7). As it does now, whenever it is taught or advocated, this commandment encountered stiff resistance. Thus, "Moses" warns against being "hard-hearted" or "tight-fisted" toward the needy. The urgency of the provision is indicated by the repeated use of an infinitive absolute, a grammatical device in Hebrew whereby the verb is intensified by repetition that cannot be replicated in translation. This grammatical device is used to intensify no fewer than six verbs in this commandment (more than in any other text), making clear that "Moses" understood that this is the most urgent and most radical of all Torah provisions.

We may pay particular attention to an apparent contradiction if we juxtapose verses 4 and 11. In verse 4, it is assured that if this commandment is performed faithfully, there will "be no one in need among you" ("the poor will cease in the land"). In verse 11, a more familiar statement asserts that "there will never cease to be some in need on the earth" ("The poor you will always have with you"). Thus, "there will be no poor" and "there will always be poor." But in fact there is no contradiction between the verses. Verse 4 states the *effectiveness* of debt cancellation; verse 11 states the *urgency* of the same policy. The predatory economy of Pharaoh works to have continuing indebtedness, in order to assure a supply of cheap labor. Israel's counterimagination insists that Pharaoh's debt-slave economy need not be practiced and is inimical to YHWH's intent for Israel.

The second provision of the "sabbatical principle" is the year of Jubilee in Leviticus 25; it provides that every forty-nine years (seven times seven), property lost in the rough-and-tumble economy will be returned to its rightful owner, because such landed property is inalienable and is not finally a tradable commodity. Thus, the autonomy of the market is severely limited in the interest of sustaining neighborly relationships.

While it is frequently contested that the proposal for a Jubilee year has no realistic future, it is important that it is reiterated as "the year of the LORD's favor" in Isaiah 61:2, a text cited by Jesus in his synagogue appearance, a citation of which he subversively declared:

Today this scripture is fulfilled in your hearing. (Luke 4:21)

It is indeed possible to trace out the Jubilee performance of Jesus in the Gospel of Luke.[10]

The Sabbath provision in the Torah is not simply a restrictive or coercive requirement. It is rather an act of bodily testimony whereby the faithful insist that economic transactions, in and of themselves, are at best penultimate and are situated in the more ultimate reality of neighborly social relationships. Seen in this way, Sabbath keeping is indeed a subversive act that asserts that Pharaoh's claims of predatory monopoly are to be resisted and are ultimately rejected.

*Creation as the basis for Sabbath keeping* (Exod. 20:11) insists that the God of covenant, and not Pharaoh, made the world and governs and sustains it. In his hubris, Pharaoh can imagine that the world is his (see Ezek. 29:3), but his claim is false. *Emancipation as the basis for Sabbath keeping* (Deut. 5:15) is an insistence that the authority of Pharaoh is limited and his claim to cheap bondaged labor is to be rejected. Sabbath is the bodily declaration that persons in the image of YHWH do not belong to Pharaoh; he is not to be obeyed or trusted or feared.

## VI. Sabbath as Testimony

Rightly understood, Sabbath is a practice of immense urgency in our contemporary political economy. It is necessary only to recognize that "Pharaoh" in the narrative is a metaphor for all predatory, confiscatory economic practice grounded in and legitimated by idolatry. As a result, we are able to see that the tenth commandment, "You shall not covet" (Exod. 20:17), is the climactic point of the Sinai covenant.[11] The covenant is an act of resistance and an alternative to the Pharaonic social system. Sabbath is the visible expression of resistance and alternative.

It is evident that our national economy in the United States (writ large as "globalization") is largely in the hands of Pharaonic interests.[12] An acquisitive oligarchy now largely manages the government, controls the media, and supports a sustained process of deregulation alongside rigged credit laws, inequitable tax arrangements, and low wages; this has resulted in a growing gap between a small party of "haves" and a large company of "have-nots" who are economically vulnerable and without leverage. As in ancient Egypt, such inequitable economics skews social relationships. "Pharaoh" is an icon for any political economy that reduces too many to low-wage jobs or no job at all, because there is no protection or safeguard against rapacious practices of the oligarchy for a workforce that is increasingly powerless. The destruction of labor unions is thus an element in the strategy of accumulation. The result is that only the "productive" are seen to have value. The "unproductive" are readily dispensable, most extremely by mass incarceration but more broadly through an arrangement of inadequate housing, unfair schools, and inaccessible health care. The indices of social health all suffer in an economy of restless anxiety in which there is no "rest" for anyone, not among the "producers," who must endlessly produce more, or among the "nonproducers," who are characteristically kept at risk.

The performance of Sabbath is an act of testimony, a powerful antidote to such a dehumanizing system of power. Practically, Sabbath is an insistence on rest for even the most vulnerable among us. Theologically, it is an insistence that the world does not belong to the predators. It belongs to the creator of heaven and earth, who intends that those in God's image cannot be reduced to commodity. This God has never intended that some should be reduced to slavery. This God has never intended that some should be reduced to commodity. This God has never intended that the earth should be plundered for the sake of limitless wealth. Sabbath keeping is a deep affirmation that all of God's creatures, human and nonhuman, should be honored in concrete and practical ways. When Jesus counsels his disciples, "Do not worry" (Luke 12:22), he surely intended that the man with "bigger barns" in the preceding parable should not be the order of the day—the restless man who never observed Sabbath and ended in death (Luke 12:16–21). Jesus surely refused endless accumulation as the purpose of life. He summoned his disciples to stand in solidarity with birds and flowers, trusting creation to know that there is enough for all. Indeed, those trusting creatures are contrasted with Solomon, Pharaoh's son-in-law, who continues, within Israel, Pharaoh's restless accumulation. Sabbath is an embrace of *the truth of the abundance* of creation against *the anxious scarcity* that reduces neighbor to threat. Sabbath is a regular, visible enactment of that alternative.

## Questions for Reflection

1. How has your understanding and practice of Sabbath changed over your life?

2. How do you understand Sabbath as a necessary opportunity to provide restfulness and refreshment both for God and for neighbor? In what way is this an act of resistance in our current political economy?

3. Brueggemann says that "life is a gift, not an accomplishment or a possession," and that "all are welcome, because their worth is not based on productivity" (pp. 90, 91). Do you inhabit communities that reflect these ideas? How so? When have you been in communities that did not adhere to these ideas? How have you seen and experienced that?

4. What are some practical ways that you can keep Sabbath as an act of testimony, embracing the abundance of creation against anxious scarcity?

Chapter 7

# Doxological Abandonment

*I*n addition to Sabbath-keeping, Israel also responds to God's grace with songs of praise. The term *hallelujah* is familiar to us from Handel's "Hallelujah Chorus" and many other contexts. It is so familiar that we may forget that it is a Hebrew word now commonly appropriated for church and popular use in our culture. (The only other Hebrew terms so widely appropriated in church use are *amen* and *shalom*.) In fact *Hallelu* is a Hebrew plural imperative of the verb *halal*, urging "Praise, all of you!" Attached to the imperative verb is the object "Yah," referring to the God of Israel, YHWH. The root word *halal* means "boast, brag," as in Jeremiah 9:23–24. Before it becomes a theological cliché, then, it might be translated "brag about Yah." The verb is thus a summons addressed to members of the community to boast of YHWH. It is a curious term, because the word voiced as a summons to praise is in fact an act of praise, so that the summons itself is an act of bragging.

This typically positive act of praise addressed to YHWH occurs in a polytheistic world of gods who are in competition with one another. Like competing cheering sections at a football game, the adherents of each god were summoned to outdo and outcheer the adherents of the other gods by louder, more vigorous acts of praise, thereby witnessing to a particular god and giving a "victory" to one god over other gods. Thus YHWH is "enthroned on the praises of Israel" (Ps. 22:3); as Israel sings praise, YHWH's throne is elevated over those of rival gods. We may imagine, then, that each act of particular praise ("Praise Yah!" or "Hallelujah!") was linked to an implied negative counterpoint ("Don't praise Baal!"). For that reason, an act of praise is not an innocuous "spiritual" act. It is rather a taking of sides for this God, against all other gods. In the Bible, other competing gods are named in various texts: Baal, Dagon, Marduk, Bel, Nebo, Asherah. In our contemporary world, the other gods might be the idols of state, race, gender, economic theory, or any preference or practice that is turned into an absolute. Whatever the case, the praise of YHWH has the effect of deabsolutizing any other candidate for "god."

## I. The Structure of Doxology

The articulation of praise in the book of Psalms characteristically has two rhetorical parts that may be arranged in various configurations and expressed in terse or in quite expansive language: the *summons* to praise and the *reasons* for praise. The simplest of praise hymns in the Psalms exhibits both elements of such rhetoric:

> Praise the LORD, all you nations!
>   Extol him, all you peoples!
> For great is his steadfast love toward us,
>   and the faithfulness of the LORD endures forever.
> Praise the LORD!
>
> Ps. 117

In verse 1, the *summons* to praise is a double imperative, "praise" (*hallelu*) and "extol." The two verbs are synonyms, both inviting boasting about YHWH. The summons is addressed to "you nations" and "you peoples," so that Israel, in its doxology, can imagine being joined in praise by many non-Israelites (or all peoples) who assent to YHWH. In doxological imagination, YHWH is taken to be not simply the God of Israel but the creator and sovereign over all peoples. It is probable that in Solomon's temple the vista of YHWH's rule was taken to be cosmic, or at least international. That scope for YHWH's rule is also echoed in the church's imagination that

> Jesus shall reign where'er the sun
> does its successive journeys run.
> Isaac Watts, 1719

In both ancient Israel and in the church, such exuberant claims run well beyond the facts on the ground.

In verse 2, the *reason* for praise is voiced: YHWH has great *steadfast love* toward us; in the parallel line, YHWH's *faithfulness* endures forever. The word pair, "steadfast love and faithfulness" offers an elemental characterization of YHWH, the God of the covenant, who is utterly reliable and trustworthy, full of grace and truth. That characterization, grounded in lived experience, is the basis for the summons to praise. The "toward us" in the first instance pertains to Israel. YHWH is faithful to Israel. But in doxological scope, Israel can proclaim that YHWH, as Creator, is faithful to all creatures, to all who worship him. The nations and the peoples are summoned to praise YHWH, who is reliable in worldly scope. In this first instance, then, divine fidelity is exhibited in Israel's life in such a way that even the nations are to boast of YHWH's fidelity to Israel. But in a second sense, even the nations can, as they will, experience that same divine fidelity in the regularity of creation as a life-giving force. The whole world is an arena for God's fidelity. In Calvin's language, the whole world is a "theatre" for the divine performance of fidelity that issues in the glory of God.

At the beginning of verse 2, the initial preposition "for" might also be translated as "because." This preposition is the connector between summons and reason—summons *because* of reason. In its praise, Israel sings back to YHWH the most important markings that YHWH has exhibited in Israel's life and in the life of the world.

This simple structure of doxology is clearest in the terse Psalm 117, together with its concluding "hallelujah" (v. 2). But the same formulation is also present in more developed and complicated psalms. Psalms 146–150 constitute a distinct collection of hymns of praise. In Psalm 146, the beginning is a summons to praise that is addressed to "my soul" (= "my self"). Verse 2 is a response to that invitation ("I will . . . I will"). The reason for such praise is given in a series of participial verbs in verses 7–9:

> who executes
> who gives
> who sets free
> who opens
> who lifts
> who loves
> who watches
> who upholds

Participial forms such as these are preferred in Israel's praise because they signify characteristic divine actions that are constantly and always being reenacted in the life of the world. YHWH is doing these acts all the time! In this recital, the name of YHWH is repeated in verses 7–9, thus accenting the peculiarity of the God addressed. The utterance of reasons (vv. 7–9) after the summons (vv. 1–2) is interrupted by a negative reflection in verses 2–5 that contrasts the "help" of the God of Jacob and the "no help" of princes and mortals. Thus the poem not only *enhances* YHWH but also *dismisses alternatives* in a polemical way. In this psalm, the reasons of verses 7–9 confirm the appropriateness of the summons of verse 1.

Next, Psalms 147 and 148 form a nice pair through which the force of doxological rhetoric is exhibited. Psalm 147 is dominated by reasons, whereas Psalm 148 abounds in summonses. Psalm 147 consists of three distinct hymns. In verses 1–6, the summons in verse 1 is followed by the connecting "for" in verse 1b. Then follow reasons for praise of YHWH, who "builds up, gathers, heals, lifts up, gives." Verses 5–6 offer a concluding formula based on the verbs just recited. In verses 7–11, we have a second psalm, introduced by a summons in verse 7. The connector at the beginning of verse 8 is implicit, though not stated. The reason for praise is that YHWH as creator gives rain, feeds birds and animals, and makes grass grow. This unit culminates with "his steadfast love" for all creatures as evidence of God's fidelity. The third hymn (Ps. 147:12–20) voices a summons in verse 12, with the connector "for" in verse 13, followed by a series of reasons concerning YHWH's actions (vv. 13–20). This list of reasons concerns every imaginable part of human experience from public to personal, from creation to history. The end of this unit identifies the special status of Israel (Jacob) with YHWH as the people who know and obey YHWH's commandments, that is, who are in faithful covenant with YHWH.

In Psalm 148, the poetry is dominated by summons, with very little space given over to reasons. The summons is addressed to all imaginable creatures, who are to join in bragging about YHWH: angels, host, sun, moon, stars, heavens, waters, sea monsters, deeps, fire, hail, snow, frost, wind, mountains, hills, fruit trees, cedars, wild animals, cattle, creeping things, birds, kings, princes, men, women, old and young!

The exuberance of this psalm is echoed in the hymn of Saint Francis, "All Creatures of Our God and King." Just like Psalm 148, Francis envisions all creatures gathered in praise around God's throne. The hymn names many creatures and then concludes with a fivefold "Alleluia." Unfortunately, the name "Yah" in this English rendering is reduced to a vowel ending, "Allelu-*ia*," a further loss of the specific name of the one to whom we sing.

Psalm 148 gives very little air time to reasons. In verse 5, the "for" acknowledges that YHWH is the creator who has fixed the order of heaven and earth. And in verse 13, the "for" exhibits YHWH's sovereignty and Israel's special status. These reasons, however, are mostly overpowered by the summons to praise, which is massive and inclusive. All creation is engaged in lively creatureliness that gladly cedes its life back to the creator in acknowledgment that life is a gift from the gracious creator. And this trend continues: in Psalm 150, the final psalm, there are no reasons at all given for praise. It is all summons!

The highly structured form of summons followed by reasons is given freer expression in Psalm 103, the best known and best loved of the hymns of praise. Here the summons is not *halal*, but *barak*, "bless." This verb has the same rhetorical function as *halal*, echoed in the fourfold "bless" in verses 20–22 at the end. The reasons are given in the participial verbs in verses 3–5. Then the poem lyrically identifies YHWH with a characteristic cluster of covenantal adjectives:

> The Lord is merciful and gracious,
>    slow to anger and abounding in steadfast love.
>                                   Ps. 103:8

From there the psalm identifies the two defining human problems, *morality* and *mortality*. Concerning *morality*, the psalmist can say:

> He does not deal with us according to our sins,
>    nor repay us according to our iniquities.
> For as the heavens are high above the earth,
>    so great is his steadfast love toward those who fear him.
>                                   vv. 10–11

Concerning *mortality*, the psalm affirms:

As for mortals, their days are like grass;
   they flourish like a flower of the field;
for the wind passes over it, and it is gone,
   and its place knows it no more.
But the steadfast love of the LORD is from everlasting to
      everlasting
   on those who fear him,
   and his righteousness to children's children.

vv. 15–17

YHWH responds to the human predicament with massive grace and generosity, more than sufficient for the wounds of guilt or the limits of death.

## II. The Practice of Praise

The practice of praise suggests five extrapolations.

First, praise is an act of imagination, not description. It sees the world through the lens of faith and dares to line out a world engaged in dialogical transactions between creator and creation. This is not the stuff witnessed by the "naked eye" or discovered by scientific analysis. This is the world seen with reference to an active, generative, engaged God who inspires and evokes praise and who, in some deep sense, depends on praise for the enhancement of divine status.

Second, hymns of praise are acts of devotion with political and polemical overtones. Their work is to engage in "world making." The very act of praise itself envisions a new world, a different world, a world alternative to the one in front of us. Indeed, hymns of praise are acts of defiance of the world that is in front of us. The work of doxology is to engage and enter another world where the real stuff concerns fidelity, obedience, and gratitude, refusing Enlightenment reason or Machiavellian politics or Friedmanian economic commitments. The singing is itself an act of transformation into a world of glad covenantalism, in which our usual anxiety-ridden way of life is overcome.

Third, the Psalms voice and are embedded in a larger narrative in which YHWH is the key character and lively agent. The Psalms only rarely exhibit the entire narrative, as in the "historical psalms."

Mostly they allude to it and take up bits and pieces of it. Regardless, the narrative in which the historical psalms are embedded and to which they witness is, first and foremost, the story of *creator and creatureliness* in which generosity and gratitude, dependence and obedience, are the order of the day. As a secondary but important subset, the Psalms also reflect the particular narrative of Israel's life that concerns both *the deliverance from Egypt* that is a paradigm for many deliverances, *the commandments of Sinai* that are in fact the shape and requirement of all creation, and *the gift of land* that brings deliverance to its promised conclusion and is where the commandments are to be lived out. Israel basks in the generous fidelity of God and sings back in dependence and gratitude, able to abandon itself in free fall into the life of YHWH. Israel exults in the historical memory of exodus-Sinai-land and knows itself in each generation to be a continuing participant in that narrative. In expositing this combination of *large* and *particular* narratives, Israel refuses both the alternative narratives of violence and the practice of nonnarrative, as though the world and our lives in it were an "eternal present" without memory or anticipation.

Fourth, doxology is the exuberant abandonment of self over to God. In singing praise, all claims for the self are given up as the self is ceded over to God. This is the same sort of ceding of self that takes place in any serious love relationship, in which the presence of the other is overwhelming and the lover wishes to hold back nothing of self from the beloved.

Such praise has narrative substance but is offered in emotive exuberance without reservation. That is why the sea "roars," the field "exults," and the trees "sing" in Psalm 96:11–12, and why the people clap and shout in Psalm 47:1. All of this is in response to the rule of God. The invitation to "bless the LORD, O my soul" is a response of the whole self (Ps. 103:1).

Such exuberant abandonment is evident when and as the church sings. But one can easily see in various assemblies that the more intellectual sophistication we have, and the more affluence we control, the less engagement there is in such exuberant abandonment, and the more is kept back in the safety of self. Doxology is toned down when we do not readily abandon our intellectual or economic control of the self, when such abandonment strikes us as embarrassing and foolish. The self-sufficient cannot and will not abandon their selves to the God of generosity and trustworthiness. Thus our self-yielding praise is a measure of our capacity to give our lives over to God, even as our toned-down doxology is a measure of our inability to yield in such grateful ways. Authentic praise "demands my soul, my life, my all" (Isaac Watts).

Fifth and last, the hymns of praise with their exuberant self-abandonment without reservation into the God of large and particular narratives are quite in contrast with what we currently call "praise songs." Contemporary praise songs, in comparison to the hymns of praise in the Psalter, seem more often than not tepid and timid, lacking narratives that are either large or particular, void of political polemic or the taking of sides, and too often end in narcissistic reductionism. Such singing constitutes not a *ceding of self,* but a *preoccupation with self* and a private religious expression that lacks depth or breadth. Such songs amount to an accommodation to an economic, political, and psychological status quo, without running any risks of being disruptive for the sake of another world.

It is clear that a great deal is at stake in doxology, when the deepest claims of faith are on exhibit. It is no wonder that the psalmist can declare:

> I will sing to the LORD as long as I live;
> I will sing praise to my God while I have being.
> Ps. 104:33

In his shrewd exposition of Mozart's music, Karl Barth wrote:

> Mozart's music is not, in contrast to that of Bach, a message, and not, in contrast to that of Beethoven, a personal confession. He does not reveal in his music any doctrine and certainly not himself. . . . Mozart does not want to say anything; he just sings and sounds. Thus he does not force anything on the listener, does not demand that he make any decisions or take any positions; he simply leaves him free.[1]

Israel claims far more than Mozart. But like Mozart, Israel in its doxologies also "sings and sounds"—but with the world hanging in the balance!

## Questions for Reflection

1. What are your reasons to praise God, grounded in your lived experience? Try listing some, using participial verbs as in Psalm 146:7–9. (I will praise God, who . . .) What covenantal adjectives would you use in a psalm of praise to God? (The Lord is . . .)

2. Besides human beings, where and when have you seen other creatures, or parts of creation, engaged in praise of God?

3. What "large and particular narratives" in your life lead you to praise God (p. 105)? Can you turn your responses to these questions into a personal psalm of praise?

4. How is your praise of God—as an act of abandoning self—reflected in your singing?

Chapter 8

# Ministry Among: The Power of Blessing

*I*n addition to Sabbath-keeping and praise-making, the church also responds to God's grace in its mission. Only now, the church has begun to rethink mission, no longer as taking the gospel to the "benighted" elsewhere. Now we talk about mission to those close at hand, near to us, those among us who are most like us. This chapter considers one biblical resource for such a shift of perspective, a shift that among other things perhaps entails a refocus in the Bible itself.

I

We may begin by considering Paul's justification for his mission to the Gentiles:

> And the scripture, foreseeing that God would justify the Gentiles by faith, declared the gospel beforehand to Abraham, saying, "All the Gentiles shall be blessed in you." For this reason, those who believe are blessed with Abraham who believed. (Gal. 3:8–9)

Paul here quotes Genesis 12:3b, part of God's initial mandate to Abraham. Oddly, Paul terms this mandate "the gospel beforehand" (*proeuangelion*), the good news of God's governance that has been known and uttered in Israel since the beginning. Paul knows that, from the outset, the gospel has been concerned with a defining and transformative relationship between the community of YHWH and all the others among whom the faithful live. In the formulation of Genesis 12:3, Paul focuses on "be blessed." I propose that we rethink our "mission among" as a mission and ministry of blessing, a way of speaking and thinking and acting that is very different from the church's usual missional rhetoric.

We may understand God's promise that Abraham will be a blessing as the culmination of a "theory of Israel" that shapes the book of Genesis in particular. First of all, blessing theology is creation theology.[1] That is, the creation texts of the Old Testament affirm that God has blessed, has ordained fruitfulness and well-being, has bestowed on the processes of creation the capacity for well-being and fulfillment of its true destiny of abundance: "God blessed them, saying, 'Be fruitful and multiply and fill the waters in the seas, and let birds multiply on the earth'" (Gen. 1:22).[2] The "force for life" has been implanted by the creator into all of creation. It is this "force for life" that constitutes the substance of blessing.

Second, on its own terms and without any dogmatic imposition of a notion of "the fall," the Genesis account of the world indicates that the defining blessing of God for the world has been resisted and distorted by the recalcitrance of the creation. As many have seen, the sequence of narratives—from Adam and Eve (Gen. 2–3), Cain and Abel (Gen. 4), the flood (Gen. 6–9), to the Tower of Babel (Gen. 11:1–9)—constitutes an inventory of recalcitrance and resistance that marks the world of the nations.[3] The outcome of these narratives is that the blessing of God for creation has been thwarted; the world is now defined by curse—perhaps curse as the direct assertion of divine threat, or perhaps simply as an outcropping of consequences of choices without any divine intrusion (see Gen. 3:14, 17; 4:11; 9:25; and differently, 8:21).[4] Either way, the "force for life" generously given by YHWH is ineffective, and the world is beset by alienation, anxiety, brutality, and the like.

And then, abruptly, comes "the gospel beforehand" to father Abraham and the communities derivative from Abraham (Jews, Christians, Muslims). "The families of the earth" (Gen. 12:3) to whom Abraham is to be a blessing are all those in Genesis 3–11 who have dropped out of the power of YHWH's blessing.[5] More specifically and concretely, the "families of the earth" are those other ethnic, social, and territorial communities with whom the ancestors—Abraham and his family—must deal on a daily basis. That is, the reference to the nations has a twofold reference, one more theological, the other quite practical as "living among" without all of the theological rhetoric. In the latter sense, the "families of the earth" are not some symbolic Other to serve theology; they are real people who dispute with Israel about land, water rights, and all the inevitable disputes of social existence.

The formula of Genesis 12:3, "the gospel beforehand," occurs as a fixed formula four more times in the ancestral narratives, clearly a quite intentional, programmatic utterance that gives shape to the disparate narratives. In 12:3, the formula is given no specificity, except that in 12:6 we are told, "at that time the Canaanites were in the land" (see 13:7). Of course, that is why it is called "the land of Canaan" (12:5–6). Whether he likes it or not, Abraham is placed among Canaanites by the God who makes promises.[6]

The formula is repeated to Abraham in 18:18. The verse is followed by the odd phrasing of verse 19: "I have chosen him, that he may charge his children and his household after him to keep the way of the LORD by doing righteousness and justice; so that the LORD may bring about for Abraham what he has promised him." This remarkable verse is the only occurrence in Genesis of the Mosaic-prophetic word pair "justice and righteousness." The couplet imports into the ancestral narrative the large social vision of Israel at its prophetic best. The nations are "blessed" when the people of Abraham practice righteousness and justice, that is, when they order social power in community-generating ways.

The third articulation to Abraham (Gen. 22:18, at the end of the story of Isaac's near-sacrifice) suggests that Abraham's way with the "nations" derives from radical obedience to God that entails deep, costly, risky sacrifice. The odd calculus of this paragraph is that Abraham, in obedience to God, risks all, with the result that the force of generative creation (blessing) will extend to all others.

The declaration of "the gospel beforehand" to Isaac in Genesis 26:4–5 reiterates the link to obedience in 22:18. Again it is the radical obedience of Abraham that counts for the nations. By linking the promise made to Isaac yet again to the obedience of his father, the ministry of blessing is rendered unmistakably intergenerational. That is, the blessing of Abraham for the nations is extended "into the third and fourth generations," and Isaac is invited to share in the alternative world of blessing.

The reiteration of the formula to Jacob (Gen. 28:14) is in the context of many other, more personal promises to Jacob. While the formulation itself adds nothing new, in the narrative that follows, even the cunning Laban can deduce that Jacob is a source of blessing in his life: "If you will allow me to say so, I have learned by divination that the LORD has blessed me because of you" (30:27).

These five formulations are a quite intentional theological shaping of the ancestral narrative. These ancestors are presented—and inside the narrative understand themselves—as a center of blessing, a concentrated locus of the "life-force" of YHWH in the world.

## II

We should be clear about this matter of blessing, for it is not a common point in our theology, let alone in our notion of mission.

First of all, blessing is understood in these narratives as a *material* process of new life that is *intrinsic* to creation and arises when the generative powers of creation function as God has intended and decreed. The emblem of the *generative powers of creation* is in the birth of children, with a patriarchal emphasis in these texts on the birth of sons. Thus the ancestral narratives are totally preoccupied with the question of arrival of the next generation, and as we have seen, in the Jacob narrative even the production of valuable animals. The blessing arises in the midst of the processes of daily life when all works well. This same celebration of generativity (expressed in quite male language) is voiced in the Psalms:

> Sons are indeed a heritage from the LORD,
>   the fruit of the womb a reward.
> Like arrows in the hand of a warrior
>   are the sons of one's youth.
> Happy is the man who has
>   his quiver full of them.
> He shall not be put to shame
>   when he speaks with his enemies in the gate.
>                            Ps. 127:3–5

> Happy is everyone who fears the LORD,
>   who walks in his ways. . . .

Your wife will be like a fruitful vine
    within your house;
your children will be like olive shoots
    around your table.
Thus shall the man be blessed
    who fears the LORD.
The LORD bless you from Zion.
    May you see the prosperity of Jerusalem
    all the days of your life.
May you see your children's children.
    Peace be upon Israel![7]

                Ps. 128:1, 3–6

The second facet of blessing important to understand is this: while blessing as life-force that produces generative, productive material prosperity is intrinsic to life-processes themselves, blessing can be *bestowed, transferred from* one party to another in an almost palpable way. Here we move into a mystery of life that does not admit of scientific or technical explanation. We are closer to a sacramental dimension of reality, whereby those who possess God's life-force in abundance can share and distribute it among others who may be deficient in what is needed for life.

We see this first of all in the family as the primal matrix of blessing that stretches intergenerationally. In Genesis 49, the old man Jacob still is master of the life-force as he had been when he was a blessing to Laban. Indeed, all through the narrative, Jacob drips with the power to enhance life. In chapter 49, he assembles his sons; he speaks a blessing over each of them, empowering them to appropriate the future that is peculiarly theirs: "All these are the twelve tribes of Israel, and this is what their father said to them when he blessed them, blessing each one of them with a suitable blessing" (Gen. 49:28; see also Deut. 33).

More contentiously and with less equanimity, this same Jacob, though younger, is a key player in Genesis 27, where the brothers dispute the blessing. Jacob "steals" the blessing from Esau, to whom it rightly belongs. Deceived Isaac blesses deceiving Jacob, giving him access to power for the future (27:27–29; note that the last phrasing of v. 29 echoes the words addressed to Abraham in Gen. 12:3). By the time Isaac finishes speaking, the blessing is assigned. It has been transmitted and cannot be recalled. This in turn produces the pathos of Esau: "'Bless me, me also, father! . . . Have you not reserved a blessing for me? . . . Have you only one blessing, father? Bless me, me also, father!' And Esau lifted up his voice and wept" (27:34–38).

Families are arenas for blessing (and cursing). Parents do bestow (and withhold) blessing on children, by gesture, word, touch, and in all kinds of subtle, less direct ways. Every family has a member(s) who is more powerful and can generate futures for others. And most families have people who are left out, like Esau.

A second arena of blessing is the priestly function, when the power of blessing is known to be concentrated in a sacred place.[8] Indeed, people come there precisely for a blessing, to have transmitted to them in sacral ways the power for life to choose a future. The best-known example, still echoed by us, is the priestly blessing of Numbers 6:24–26, whereby Aaron and his sons bestow upon Israel a future of grace and peace. (It is too bad, in my judgment, that in much of the church the priestly authority to bless has been trivialized, likely because the priests themselves are embarrassed by such power or do not believe in it, and so the benediction becomes, all too often, nothing more than a signing off with "Good luck.")

The ancestral narrative, playing upon the claims of *family* and *priests*, makes the claim that the power of blessing is concentrated in this community of faith, but that power of blessing is not only for Israel. It is rather "by you" that the power of blessing shall be transmitted to and for the others who have, since their embrace of curse, been deficient in the power to choose a prosperous future.

## III

Insofar as this line of interpretation is useful, it needs to be understood that I am urging a quite different notion of "ministry among." It is to be observed that Abraham and his kin never directly confront the nations with their faith, never seek to recruit or convert. Rather, the power of blessing is a free gift offered to the nations, as it has been graciously entrusted to Israel. The purpose of blessing is not to enhance Israel, nor even to accent the importance of YHWH. It is rather that the community should "work," as more and more people are included in the power of blessing, and so are freed of the dread, deathly force of curse. I do not imagine that this is all that can be said about "ministry among," but it is an important motif that may stop well short of a desperate triumphalism that understands mission as imposition.

Thus I propose that "ministry among" consists, as it did for the ancestors, in being visibly available with the life-force of a viable future of shalom that will energize and evoke participation by others who still hold to other ideological loyalties. This reconsideration of mission may be illumined by observing two thematic contrasts.

First, as many scholars have observed, especially Jewish scholars, the theological mind-set and perspective of Genesis is very different from the Moses–Joshua materials that follow. The latter are conflictual, violent, and aimed at domination.[9] It is plausible that in the long run, the dominant missional rhetoric of the church is derived from this conflictual tradition that aims at victory. By contrast, the ancestral narratives in Genesis are largely absent of such conflict and therefore do not aim at triumph or engage in violence. What text we read makes a huge difference about the model of mission we embrace!

Second, the *blessing theology* that pervades the ancestral narratives is creation theology that is concerned with the full functioning of generativity that has been ordained in creation, so that the belated fruitfulness of Israel's mothers is a continuation of the fruitfulness of creation. By contrast, *the redemption traditions* of Moses and Joshua are preoccupied with liberation, emancipation, and transformation, a much more confrontational, disruptive perspective. I understand that one cannot finally separate creation from redemption. But one can make very different accents. I suspect that to avoid the missional triumphalism that has done so much damage and that now feeds the Christian right, an accent on the generosity of creation is a way to refocus mission.

While it is beyond my competence, I suggest that the tension in these two thematic contrasts resembles the tension between Romans–Galatians on the one hand, and Colossians–Ephesians on the other, insofar as the latter think primarily in terms of the mystery of creation. It is also not unimportant that Colossians and Ephesians are not a hotbed of doctrinal dispute or of evangelical machismo, as Romans and Galatians tend to be.

## IV

The two accents on *material-intrinsic* and *bestowal and transference* invite us to think about the church in North America as a community in which God's life-force for a viable future is concentrated. That concentration of God's life-force may be shared with "Gentiles" outside the community who will be blessed. Earlier I suggested that the power of curse is characterized by *alienation, anxiety*, and *brutality*. I am not sure that those are the best words, and I did not linger long over choosing them. The reader may think of better terms by which to characterize the deep distortion that now marks civil society in North America. I have in mind the unchecked creep of market logic that reduces everything to a commodity and the ceaseless pursuit of commodities that stops at nothing to achieve "the most." This disorder has many faces—consumerism, war on the poor, mass incarceration, militarism, a fascination with technology, toxic Christian nationalism, white supremacism, domestic abuse, and more.

Behind all of this deep social alienation, I suspect is the anxiety that there is not enough—not enough for retirement, not enough for education, not enough for medical coverage, not enough for our children, not enough for our community, not enough for our nation, not enough for our church—so we are endlessly under threat. The deeply felt scarcity all around us is a function of an atheism that denies the generosity of the Creator and doubts the abundance of creation. Our North American civic culture is cursed by a sense of scarcity, in which the neighbor question evaporates, and erstwhile neighbors are seen to be at best inconveniences, more likely as threats.

In the midst of that fearful, feverish pursuit of "enough" sits the church, with its news, its sacraments, its priestly power to bless. The church—the local, organized, visible church—is *a place of abundance*, precisely because in its fidelity the church continues to count on and live from the endless self-giving of God the creator. Our prayers and our hymns and our texts all attest to the goodness and inexhaustible generosity of God, "who by the power at work within us is able to accomplish abundantly far more than all we can ask or imagine" (Eph. 3:20).

This concentration (not monopoly or property) of abundance sits in the midst of the power of curse. It refuses to give in, even though deep among us the seductions of alienation, anxiety, and brutality are at work. It is the primal liturgical task of the church now, I believe, to insist that we will not give in, even though, as always, the power of curse is more compelling and more palpable than is the power of blessing.

## V

1. The gospel is *the story* of miraculous abundance. The stories we tell—perhaps even at "children's time"—are about the history of blessing that is put together one episode at a time, that all together tells about abundance that breaks out among us inexplicably. Abraham and Sarah wondered about the power of blessing, and were left in Genesis 18:14 with the haunting question: "Is anything too wonderful for the LORD?" The tradition that bears the gospel asserts that nothing is beyond the creator who blesses. Nothing is impossible! Nothing is too hard! The God who permeates this counterhistory of blessing is a giver. So Paul taunts his detractors: "What do you have that you did not receive? And if you received it, why do you boast as if it were not a gift?" (1 Cor. 4:7). It's all gift!

2. The mission insists on *gestures of charity and generosity*. That is what the church does best . . . modest, visible, intentional acts of neighborliness that entail some giving of self for another. We take that so for granted, and it is often more habitual than it is intentional. But we should at least notice that people caught in cycles of alienation, anxiety, and brutality can give nothing and can notice nothing of abundance. Not to be dismissed are the endless works of canned goods, care packages, Christmas gifts and soup kitchens and clothing drives and tutoring and shelters, mostly done by nameless saints. All these are overt gestures that refuse to concede defining authority to the power of curse. Here and there, in face-to-face contact, concentrated blessing is shared, and people receive power for life.

3. The mission consists in *public actions* that create budgets, policies, and institutions that become channels of blessing. Under the cursed ideology of "privatization," our society seems bent on dismantling everything it can get its hands on. The mandate to

Abraham concerning "justice and righteousness," however, makes clear that the power of blessing is not an in-house, church thing to be restricted to acts of charity. Blessing has a public face, for the entire tradition of Israel understands that blessing is a public matter, too urgent to be left intimate. And so the great issues of peace, justice, health, education, housing, and jobs are all facets of blessing "by you."

# VI

Much of the ministry of Jesus is the enactment of abundance in contexts gone sour with deprivation. He is presented in the Gospels as a bodied person who exudes blessing. In Luke 8:44–45, the woman who had tried many failed alternatives came to him: "She came up behind him and touched the fringe of his clothes, and immediately her hemorrhage stopped." Jesus of course noticed: "Who touched me? . . . Someone touched me; for I noticed that power had gone out from me." She is immediately healed, because she had come into contact with his futuring power; she is restored to fullness of life. He does not recruit her or even invite her in. He only blesses her.

In the preceding chapter, John the Baptist wonders about Jesus' identity (Luke 7:20). Jesus' answer is void of explicit theological claim: "The blind receive their sight, the lame walk, the lepers are cleansed, the deaf hear, the dead are raised, the poor have good news brought to them. And blessed is anyone who takes no offense at me" (vv. 22–23). The power to bless exudes from his body and makes all things new. John does not get a neat theological formula; but he now knows everything he needs to know.

We are the people who trail behind Jesus in the history of blessing. What a claim for the church, to be known as the people of limitless resources shared with no restraint, limitless because the abundance of the Creator is so trusted that we are persuaded out of our calculating fearfulness! The amazing thing is that when "power goes out," it is more than replenished by the gracious Creator, who continues to bless. The long history is that where there has been this kind of generosity, "loaves abound" . . . as well as members!

# Questions for Reflection

1. Do you agree that nations are "blessed" when the people of God "order social power in community-generating ways" (p. 111)? Can you think of any specific examples?

2. How have you experienced family as an arena of blessing in intergenerational ways? Do you recall giving a blessing to or receiving a blessing from someone in another generation? If you could speak a blessing to a family member in a different generation, what might you say?

3. What benedictions/blessings are you familiar with at the close of worship? How are they more than *a signing off with "Good luck"*?

4. What does a "ministry among" that keeps at its core blessing, abundance, and public actions look like in your faith community? Or what could it look like?

Chapter 9

# The Impossible Possibility of Forgiveness

*T*he practice that the church most often associates with grace is forgiveness. Yet forgiveness is a theological possibility that needs to be framed in intelligible and critical ways. To that end, this chapter will consider three questions that the church might ponder concerning the proclamation and experience of the good news of forgiveness. For each question I will suggest how it is processed and resolved in Old Testament texts.

## I. What Makes Forgiveness Impossible?

*"Sometime the hating has to stop"[1]*

Forgiveness remains impossible when life is parsed in the mode of "deeds-consequences," when it is thought and experienced that deeds have an unbreakable, tight, predictable connection to consequences that arise from them. While this mode of thinking can be imagined positively, that good deeds evoke blessings, most often this assumption is understood and accented negatively, that bad deeds inevitably and inescapably produce negative consequences, whether by automatic results (e.g., smoking causes cancer) or by punishing authorities that guarantee moral order (e.g., three strikes and you are out). Because the calculus of deeds and consequences cannot be broken or violated, forgiveness is impossible. One must live with the consequences of one's deeds . . . to perpetuity!

This notion of "deeds-consequences" is pervasive in the Old Testament (and is not absent from the New Testament but is reflected, for example, in the question posed in John 9:2: "Who sinned, this man or his parents, that he was born blind?").[2] First, it is the theological assumption of the theology of Deuteronomy, the dominant theology of the Old Testament. Obedience to the commandments yields well-being; disobedience yields covenant curses (see Deut. 28:1–68).

> See, I have set before you today life and prosperity, death and adversity. If you obey the commandments of the LORD your God that I am commanding you today, by loving the LORD your God, walking in his ways, and observing his commandments, decrees, and ordinances, then you shall live and become numerous, and the LORD your God will bless you in the land that you are entering to possess. But if your heart turns away and you do not hear, but are led astray to bow down to other gods and serve them, I declare to you today that you shall perish; you shall not live long in the land that you are crossing the Jordan to enter and possess. (Deut. 30:15–18)

The disproportionate accent on curses in chapter 28 indicates that the force of this double "if-then" arrangement is on the negative.

Second, this same "deeds-consequences" construct is the structural assumption of the recurring prophetic speeches of judgment that regularly consist in an *indictment* of Torah disobedience and a *sentence* that follows from old covenant curses.[3] The two are characteristically connected by a "therefore" that allows for both automatic outcomes and divine agency:

> Hear the word of the LORD, O people of Israel;
>     for the LORD has an indictment against the inhabitants of the land.
> There is no faithfulness or loyalty,
>     and no knowledge of God in the land.
> Swearing, lying, and murder,
>     and stealing and adultery break out;
>     bloodshed follows bloodshed.
> *Therefore* the land mourns,
>     and all who live in it languish;
> together with the wild animals
>     and the birds of the air,
>     even the fish of the sea are perishing.
>                                                      Hos. 4:1–3

> Its rulers give judgment for a bribe,
>     its priests teach for a price,
>     its prophets give oracles for money;
> yet they lean on the LORD and say,
>     "Surely the LORD is with us!
> No harm shall come upon us."
> *Therefore* because of you
>     Zion shall be plowed as a field;
> Jerusalem shall become a heap of ruins,
>     and the mountain of the house a wooded height.
>
> Mic. 3:11–12

The prophets, reflective of the tradition of Deuteronomy, assume a close connection between deeds and consequences, between covenantal disobedience and covenantal curse. The "divine therefore" permits connections to be made that might otherwise elude us.

Third, the same connection of deeds and consequences is the tacit assumption of the wisdom teaching in the book of Proverbs:[4]

> A slack hand causes poverty,
>     but the hand of the diligent makes rich.
> . . . . . . . . . . . . . . . . . . . . . . . . . . . . . .
> The wage of the righteous leads to life,
>     the gain of the wicked to sin.
> . . . . . . . . . . . . . . . . . . . . . . . .
> The fear of the LORD prolongs life,
>     but the years of the wicked will be short.
> . . . . . . . . . . . . . . . . . . . . . . . . . . . . . .
> The righteous will never be removed,
>     but the wicked will not remain in the land.
>
> (Prov. 10:4, 16, 27, 30)

It is also the governing subject of the dispute between Job and his friends. The God of the whirlwind has no interest in such a calculus, but it nonetheless dominates the book of Job as an heir to the book of Proverbs.

Thus the *Deuteronomic, prophetic*, and *sapiential* traditions all agree on this basic assumption. That assumption, on the one hand, operates as *social control* to motivate people to "get it right." On the other hand, it serves to assure a *moral coherence* to reality, so that one's actions are important and significant in shaping the future:

"What you sow, you reap!" This same assumption is pervasive in popular religion and in civic life among us.

First, it is the basis of much *right-wing religion* that preaches "hell, fire, and damnation" that frightens people into a "moral life." Wrong living will evoke long-term punishment that is inescapable. Indeed, many who have long since left such religion continue to hold such assumptions.

Second, that same assumption has been transposed in powerful ways from religion to *market ideology*, so that obedience to the mandates of the market brings economic preference; those who do not produce endlessly may be left behind with unforgivable, intractable debt. Those who do not shop and consume continually, moreover, are "letting down our side." The pressure of getting kids into the right preschool and building kids' "dossiers" with soccer and dance lessons are all a part of the "deeds-consequences" pressure of the market. If one does not "perform" adequately, one will surely "suffer the consequences."

Third, I dare imagine that the same pressure, less closely articulated, permeates notions of citizenship among *good liberals* who perform their duty in generous, engaged civic ways, because like Job they do not "fear God for nothing" (Job 1:9). Indeed I imagine that the same unspoken assumption operates in some duty-propelled pastors, who must endlessly "prove themselves," and even in seminary teachers, who must endlessly produce one more published article!

The assumption behind these performance-based forms of faith is that God's world is organized in an inexorable way that yields rewards and punishments. This assumption interpreted the major crisis of the Old Testament, the destruction of Jerusalem, as divine punishment for long-term disobedience to Torah. The long telling of royal history in the books of Kings concerns the demise and failure of Jerusalem, its monarchy and temple, that effectively ended the history of Israel in the exile with its shame, deportation, and displacement (see 2 Kgs. 24:13–25:21; Jer. 52:12–30). The long prayer of Ezra (Neh. 9:6–37) and the long recital of Psalm 106 attest to this long-term failure.

Fourth, I suggest that in contemporary popular culture, the defining anthem of this theology is "Santa Claus Is Coming to Town":

> He's gonna find out
> Who's naughty and nice. . . .

He knows if you've been bad or good,
So be good for goodness sake!

In teasing good humor the song is in fact a form of social control with the prospect of "coal" for poor performances that are never forgiven. This applies not only to "our kids" but to many adults as well!

## II. What Makes Forgiveness Possible?

*"There can be no reconciliation . . . if there has not been a sundering"[5]*

According to the theology of "deeds-consequences," the history of Israel would properly have come to an end in the destruction of Jerusalem. That "end" is voiced in the grief of the book of Lamentations:

> The roads to Zion mourn;
>     for no one comes to the festivals;
> all her gates are desolate,
>     her priests groan;
> her young girls grieve,
>     and her lot is bitter . . .
> because the LORD has made her suffer
>     for the multitude of her transgressions. . . .
> [S]o I say, "Gone is my glory,
>     and all that I had hoped for from the LORD."
>                     Lam. 1:4–5; 3:18

Hope is gone! Deeds have received consequences. Disobedience has evoked covenant curses. Finis! No forgiveness! No possible future!

The wonder of the Old Testament, of Judaism, and consequently of Christian faith, is that this turns out not to be the end. There is a continuation that is grounded in forgiveness. So the poet in Lamentations can continue:

> But this I call to mind,
>     and therefore I have hope:
> The steadfast love of the LORD never ceases,
>     his mercies never come to an end;

> they are new every morning;
>   great is your faithfulness.
> 3:21–23

Continuation is grounded in divine steadfast love, faithfulness, and mercy, the "big three" of gracious covenantal relationship.

What makes forgiveness possible is the astonishing readiness of God to reach beyond deeds-consequences, to restore and sustain the relationship that had by all proper measure been terminated in disobedience. It is this inexplicable reach of God beyond "deeds-consequences" that makes forgiveness possible. We may see this in two texts that are likely preexilic. In Exodus 34, after the golden calf incident and the hard negotiations on the part of Moses, Moses utters a final, desperate petition to YHWH:

> Although this is a stiff-necked people, pardon our iniquity and our sin, and take us for your inheritance. (Exod. 34:9)

The answer to the prayer is not certain, which is why the prayer is an act of risky hope. The divine answer, however, opens the future:

> I hereby make a covenant. Before all your people I will perform marvels, such as have not been performed in all the earth or in any nation; and all the people among whom you live shall see the work of the LORD; for it is an awesome thing that I will do with you. (v. 10)

God moves beyond indignation over the golden calf to generate a new future based in forgiveness.

In Hosea 11:5–7, God is in a rant against recalcitrant Israel. But then, in mid-rant, YHWH interrupts YHWH's own speech with self-questioning wonderment:

> How can I give you up, Ephraim?
>   How can I hand you over, O Israel?
> How can I make you like Admah?
>   How can I treat you like Zeboiim?
> Hos. 11:8a

YHWH comes in that instant to realize that YHWH has no inclination to enact fierce anger, but turns the rant into a reach of compassion:

My heart recoils within me;
　　my compassion grows warm and tender.
I will not execute my fierce anger;
　　I will not again destroy Ephraim;
for I am God and no mortal,
　　the Holy One in your midst,
　　and I will not come in wrath.

vv. 8b–9

That divine reach is inexplicable, but it is the indispensable act of God that makes new life possible for Israel.

In exile, when "deeds-consequences" reaches its completion in punishment and all hope is lost, there is a surge of divine forgiveness for Israel, grounded in God's reach to generate newness.

First, in the tradition of Isaiah, we have had a long condemnation of society in a series of "woes" (Isa. 5:8–24). But now, at the end of Second Isaiah, the poet has God make a bid for restoration:

Seek the LORD while he may be found.
　　call upon him while he is near; . . .
let them return to the LORD, that he may have mercy on them,
　　and to our God, for he will abundantly pardon.

Isa. 55:6–7

The operational word is *pardon*. That God's ways are "higher," as verse 9 declares, may thus mean that they supersede "deeds-consequences," in order to make new life possible. What follows in verses 12–13 is an imagined, unexpected glorious procession home, made possible by the God who has broken the tired, killing grip of deeds-consequences.

Second, the tradition of Jeremiah has at length castigated Jerusalem and arrived in 19:11 at the harsh ultimate judgment:

So I will break this people and this city, as one breaks a potter's vessel, so that it can never be mended.

The verb "mended" means "healed," which puts Jerusalem beyond restitution. And yet, when we reach "the Book of Comfort" in Jeremiah 30–31, there is "grace in the wilderness" (31:2) and "everlasting love" (31:3) that culminates in "new covenant" (31:31–34).

That famous passage ends: "I will forgive their iniquity, and remember their sin no more" (31:34). "Deeds-consequences" causes us to remember our failure longer than God remembers. Newness in Israel is grounded in YHWH's readiness to break the cycle of disobedience-punishment with a generous act of forgiveness whereby old calculations about consequences are removed from reckoning. The assertion of forgiveness is reiterated by the prophet:

> I will restore the fortunes of Judah and the fortunes of Israel, and rebuild them as they were at first. I will cleanse them from all the guilt of their sin against me, and I will forgive all the guilt of their sin and rebellion against me. (Jer. 33:7–8)

Third, the prophet Ezekiel, in one of his best-known passages, hews to the line of deed-consequences:

> If a man is righteous and does what is lawful and right . . . follows my statutes, and is careful to observe my ordinances, acting faithfully—such a one is righteous; he shall surely live, says the Lord GOD. . . . But if the wicked turn away from all their sins that they have committed and keep all my statutes and do what is lawful and right, they shall surely live; they shall not die. (Ezek. 18:5, 9, 21)

Later on, however, Ezekiel must have concluded that such a "turn" is not possible. In a torrent of unconditional divine promises, Israel will be transformed by YHWH's reach for new beginnings:

> I will take you from the nations, and gather you from all the countries, and bring you into your own land. I will sprinkle clean water upon you, and you shall be clean from all your uncleannesses, and from all your idols I will cleanse you. A new heart I will give you, and a new spirit I will put within you; and I will remove from your body the heart of stone and give you a heart of flesh. I will put my spirit within you, and make you follow my statutes and be careful to observe my ordinances. (36:24–27)

It is spectacularly the case that all three "major prophets" have God moved from "deeds-consequences" that issues in punishment to a fresh reach beyond to new possibility. That of course is the point of possibility. I do not think, however, that point has force unless and until we are clear about the weight of "deeds-consequences" in our lives. It is precisely in the hopeless outcome of

"deeds-consequences," which generates fear, self-hatred, and endless pressure, that the divine reach of compassion and forgetfulness
has transformative power, as it did for ancient Israel. This means
that God

- reaches beyond hell, fire, and damnation to create new life;
- reaches beyond self-hatred and shame with tender mercy that
  vetoes such hatred;
- reaches beyond the defeats and hopeless pressures to "catch-up"
  in the market economy in order to validate those "left behind";
- reaches beyond the pressure of liberals with their endless commitments to enter into an unbelievable Sabbath rest.

It is not easy for those of us inured to "deeds-consequences" to
accept such a reach. I think, however, that the preachable point is
that such a reach is not easy for God either. God, so the tradition
attests, is—like us—inured to "deeds-consequences" and to acute
self-regard that will not be mocked by casual defiance or prideful
recalcitrance. Forgiveness, as we may imagine, requires nothing less
than God's capacity to resituate God's own life outside the orbit of
deeds-consequences. This is why, I judge, that it is exactly in the
exile that we begin to see new maternal images for God. God must
move in new ways if the lethal cycle of deeds-consequences is to be
nullified. As a result, the congregation might be led to consider how
forgiveness has been experienced, and who has been able to step
outside "deeds-consequences" to allow for the slippage that makes
new life possible.

Since we pray, "Forgive us our sins as we forgive those who sin
against us," we might be invited to consider how we ourselves might
step outside "deeds-consequences" for the sake of forgiveness. If as
James Joyce asserts there can be no reconciliation without sundering,
we may ask, "What must be sundered?" The answer is that God's
way of governing needed to be sundered. And so with us, what must
be sundered is our self-concept, our self-presentation, our old habits of holding grudges and keeping score and harboring long-term
resentments.

After the phrasing of the prayer, it is likely that we cannot *receive*
forgiveness unless we are in something of a posture of *enacting* forgiveness. That is, we cannot entertain God's reach beyond

"deeds-consequences" unless we ourselves are alive to the possibility of such a reach.

All of our conventional habits of grudge preservation are called to account. Such a sundering may variously pertain to:

- long-held familial alienations
- old habits of quarreling in the congregation
- old party conversations that regularly excommunicate "red" or "blue" folks in the community
- old stereotypes of race, gender, class
- old resentment of the "undeserving poor"
- old caricatures of those "not like us," for example, Jews or Muslims

The history of life beyond the habits that "cannot be mended" requires such sundering.

## III. What Does Forgiveness Make Possible?

When I develop a mindset of forgiveness, rather than a mindset of grievance, I don't just forgive a particular act; I become a more forgiving person.

With a grievance mindset, I look at the world and see what is wrong. When I have a forgiveness mindset, I start to see the world not through grievance but through gratitude. (Desmond Tutu and Mpho Tutu)[6]

The ancient "assurance of pardon" anticipated that one forgiven would be able to lead a "godly, righteous, and sober life," that is, a life in sync with the God who forgives. Forgiveness is an emancipation from the fear, shame, guilt, and self-hatred to a new freedom:

1. It is a break beyond hell, fire, and damnation to be one's true self.
2. It is a break beyond the claims of market productivity to be rather than to do.
3. It is a break beyond liberal "duty" to bask in a truly accepted, acceptable life.

Forgiveness is an emancipation that lifts all the weight of "deeds-consequences" and permits a "lightness of being." A genuinely forgiven person is one who is deeply and gladly attached to the forgiver, not "indebted" but grateful.

In the Old Testament prophets, what comes from forgiveness is the capacity to imagine, host, and perform concrete and specific newnesses that are impossible except for forgiveness. The preacher thus may ponder that what follows from forgiveness is "that all things are possible."

First, in the book of Isaiah, Second Isaiah ends, as noted, with promised pardon (Isa. 55:6–9) and joyous homecoming (55:12–13). After that, the book of Isaiah portrays a reimagined society that is now possible. Chapter 56 imagines inclusiveness for those most eagerly excluded: eunuchs and foreigners. The new prospect is that "my house shall be called a house of prayer for all peoples" (56:7).

In chapter 58, a new social fabric is proposed that will make possible a common good shared between haves and have-nots:

> Is not this the fast that I choose:
>     to loose the bonds of injustice,
>     to undo the thongs of the yoke,
> to let the oppressed go free,
>     and break every yoke?
> Is it not to share your bread with the hungry,
>     and bring the homeless poor into your house;
> when you see them naked, to cover them,
>     and not to hide yourself from your own kin?
> Isa. 58:6–7

Most especially, in anticipation of "I have a Dream," 65:17–25 can hold in purview a new Jerusalem, a new urban ordering of social power, in which they "shall not hurt or destroy on all my holy mountain" (65:25). An unforgiven urban economy will systematically hurt and will programmatically destroy. But not now! Now urban newness is possible!

Second, the book of Jeremiah is rooted in the old Torah memory of Sinai via the tradition of Deuteronomy. When Jeremiah comes to imagine what is possible via forgiveness, he imagines a new covenant, in which there will be glad acceptance of Torah commandments, not as coercion, but as a body of teaching that will bring life. The anticipation of a new covenant is a marvel, because Jeremiah can recall broken covenant, a brokenness that recurs but that reaches back all the way to broken covenant caused by the golden calf (Jer. 11:10). But because of forgiveness, restored covenant is possible, and with it a covenantal community and a covenantal ordering of social power. Implicit in "new covenant" is a new neighborly economy that specializes in forgiveness of debts, not a bad thing to think about as public policy in a society that leaves students with unbearable debts and that generates and accepts as normal a permanent underclass.

Third, Ezekiel by contrast is rooted in the priestly tradition reflected in the book of Leviticus, which is preoccupied with holiness. He has earlier imagined the departure of God's glory from Jerusalem and its temple because God could not remain in a place of profanation (Ezek. 9–10). Ezekiel imagines that in time to come there will be a new temple (Ezek. 40–48). YHWH will return in glory to reside permanently in the new temple. This act of prophetic imagination is counter to all the facts on the ground of Israel's failed holiness. Ezekiel's temple is not primarily about architecture. It is about the readiness of God to be with God's people and to invest their common life with holiness. It is forgiveness that makes the divine presence possible in Israel. This God who will come in glory will, in time to come, be shepherd of Israel:

> I myself will be the shepherd of my sheep, and I will make them lie down, says the Lord GOD. I will seek the lost, and I will bring back the strayed, and I will bind up the injured, and I will strengthen the weak, but the fat and the strong I will destroy. I will feed them with justice. (34:15–16)

It is worth considering this vision of a new temple and a new sense of divine presence in a society like ours. Glory has indeed departed from among us in the collapse of US exceptionalism, precisely because profanation is emphatic in our trivializing of common life and the reduction of everything and everyone to a commodity. But now, forgiven, new temple and new presence!

## IV. Conclusion

It is useful, I think, to give narrative body to the crisis of forgiveness. Thus the sequence I propose in the Old Testament is:

1. the symmetry of "deeds-consequences"
2. the reach beyond "deeds-consequences" symmetry in generosity that sunders old patterns and old assumptions
3. lightness of being that makes all things possible

It will occur to some readers familiar with my work that this sequence is yet another articulation of my typology in the book of Psalms of "orientation, disorientation, and new orientation."[7] Of course the "old orientation" of "deeds-consequences" is on all counts powerful among us and will continue to be so. It is, I propose, a disorientation in God's own life with the emergence of pathos-filled solidarity that causes a genuine break in old patterns of governance. The performance of that solidarity makes all things new, a possibility never possible under the aegis of "deeds-consequences."

I am of course aware that this dramatic sequence is acted out many times in the narratives that cluster around Jesus. It is reflected, moreover, in the most normative "three-point sermon" of sin–salvation–new life, the original classic form of the three-point sermon, always the same three points. But in the sequence that I have traced, the first accent is not explicitly on "sin." It concerns, rather, the theological-moral assumption of "deeds-consequences" that produces a graceless world. This dramatic sequence is definitional for the narrative of Jesus and in the faith of ancient Israel for the destiny of Jerusalem. The same drama is many times performed in the life of a congregation. I hazard that many people come to church with the assumptions of "deeds-consequences." The best hope (and fear!) is that the claim of "deeds-consequences" will be broken, hope because we yearn for reconciliation, fear because such a break signifies the eclipse of an old order of certitude. The reach beyond such certitude feels to some like a plunge into unbearable relativism.

Thus three questions arise:

1. *What makes forgiveness impossible?* It is the grip of "deeds-consequences" that allows no "out."
2. *What makes forgiveness possible?* It is the inexplicable reach of generous graciousness beyond "deeds-consequences."
3. *What does forgiveness make possible?* Everything congruent with the forgiver.

These are questions that belong primarily (not exclusively) to the gospel community. What a way to imagine the church, a community that is preoccupied with these questions (and answers) that eventually concern both our personal destiny and our social, communal possibility! I suggest that preaching forgiveness is not simply a declaration of God's love and grace, but it is a close attentiveness to costly sundering that makes new life possible. It is a wonder to imagine God's readiness to be sundered for the sake of newness. It is an equal wonder to consider our readiness for such a break in our way of being present in the world.

My title, "Impossible Possibility" is a play on the phrasing of Kierkegaard. The phrase is exactly to the point. We know in our habitual practices about the stubborn impossibility of forgiveness. We only rarely experience the way that the impossibility of forgiveness becomes possible. But that is the primal truth of our faith. God turns that impossibility to possibility, and from that possibility all other things become possible. This is a truth that our society little suspects. But we know better. We constitute a body that is resolved to receive and embrace this truth, along with the freedom and courage for the "reach beyond" that comes with sundering.

## Questions for Reflection

1. Where do you see the idea of "deeds-consequences" at work in contemporary culture? How has it been a part of your own life?

2. Do you agree that "it is likely that we cannot *receive* forgiveness unless we are in something of a posture of *enacting* forgiveness" (p. 129)? What does that mean for us and our neighbors as we pray, "Forgive us our sins, as we forgive those who sin against us"?

3. Can you write an assurance of pardon for worship that is shaped by and/or articulates Brueggemann's idea of forgiveness as an impossible possibility?

4. What new ideas about your congregation's call to live as God's forgiven people does this chapter raise for you?

Chapter 10

# A Myriad of "Truth
# and Reconciliation" Commissions

*W*e are, we confess, saved by grace: delivered by God's good
power from the power of evil; rescued by God's generosity from the
destructiveness of our own sin. Most of us, schooled in Paul, will
readily affirm that that rescue and deliverance are all God's work,
not ours:

> We may be surprised, however, to find in Paul's letters virtu-
> ally no use of certain words we often employ in connection with
> righting what is wrong. When he speaks to human beings of their
> wickedness, should he not call on them to *repent*! And should he
> not say that, after repenting, they can be assured of the peace and
> rightness that comes with *forgiveness*! Yet, in all of his references
> to the righting of what has gone wrong, Paul makes no significant
> reference to repentance and forgiveness.[1]

The gift of new life is fully accomplished by God, so the themes of
repentance and forgiveness leave little to be said.

Except, the reception of the free gift from God is not easy, and the
truth of that grace is not cheap. For that reason, every pastor knows
that there are disciplines that belong to the reception of God's grace,
tasks inescapably entailed in the reality of forgiveness.

I

For the most part, what the psalmist says here is not true:

> Against you, you alone, have I sinned,
>   and done what is evil in your sight.
> Ps. 51:4

It was not true even for David, to whom the superscription attributes this psalm; he had sinned against God to be sure, but also against Uriah and Bathsheba (2 Sam. 12:9). Characteristically our distorted lives violate our relationships both with God and with neighbor. That is why, along with the "first commandment," there is always a "second . . . like it" (Matt. 22:34–39). As violation of Torah characteristically involves both God and neighbor, so the work of forgiveness relates to both God and neighbor.

I take it that this double fruit of sin and the commensurate double task of receiving forgiveness were in Jesus' purview in his teaching in the Sermon on the Mount:

> So when you are offering your gift at the altar, if you remember that your brother or sister has something against you, leave your gift there before the altar and go; first be reconciled to your brother or sister, and then come and offer your gift. (Matt 5:23–24)

A "gift at the altar" might indeed be a fresh approach to God, an acknowledgment of God's rule, an articulation of gratitude for right or restored relationship with God. One cannot come to such a gift-giving enterprise with God, however, until there is reconciliation with the neighbor who has a grievance.

In the teaching of Jesus, the term "reconcile" is left uninflected. We may take it to mean, whether by word or by act, to right a wrong. Such a righting of a wrong clears the way to continue the journey to the altar for gift-giving to God as an act of acknowledgment, an articulation of gratitude, and a restoration of that relationship that has been breached. The journey interrupted by neighbor reality, when completed, leaves one in the position to love God and to love neighbor afresh. There is no question in the teaching of Jesus, any more than in the theology of Paul, that the gift brought to the altar will be accepted. The path to that wondrous enactment of gift, however, is via reconciliation with the neighbor.

## II

I think it probable that the teaching of Jesus cited above is rooted in the priestly instruction of Leviticus 6:1–7 (in Hebrew, 5:20–26). That priestly teaching, amid general and detailed instructions about sacrifices, provides guidance in the priestly horizon about the path to reconciliation. The beginning of the teaching is noteworthy:

> When any of you sin and commit a trespass against the LORD . . .
> (Lev. 6:2a)

Here is a distortion against God that causes a skewed relationship with God. But the text promptly continues:

> by deceiving a neighbor . . . (v. 2b)

The connection between *transgression against God* and *deceiving a neighbor* is by a single particle, a one-letter Hebrew conjunction, suggesting that the second fills out the substance of the first. Distorted relationship with God is accomplished *by* distorted relationship with neighbor.

The affront against the neighbor, which constitutes a trespass "against the LORD," is a matter of economics. The examples Leviticus lists include deposit, pledge, robbery, fraud, and something lost and found and lied about. Sins against neighbor that constitute transgression against God are not emotive or private or romantic matters. They concern, first of all, hard-nosed materialism about economic transactions of a systemic kind that block communion with God. The sin is thus double-edged—surprise, surprise!—God and neighbor! Notice, moreover, that the sin is not twofold. It is one act that affronts both God and neighbor.

Given such an analysis of sin, it will not surprise us that the antidote to such sin is also double-edged and requires the completion of two tasks in turn, the same two tasks identified by Jesus in his teaching on reconciliation. The first task is a full acknowledgment of what has been done against the neighbor, the capacity to recognize violation of the neighbor for what it is, and a resolve to overcome that violation:

> When you have sinned and realize your guilt, and would restore
> what you took by robbery or by fraud or the deposit that was com-
> mitted to you, or the lost thing that you found, or anything else
> about which you have sworn falsely . . . (Lev. 6:4–5a)

The agenda of reconciliation matches the detail of the affront given
in verses 2–3: robbery, fraud, deposit, lost thing. The operative
words are "would restore." The verb "restore" means to return to
the owner what is rightly the property of the owner that has been
inappropriately taken. Hebrew lacks any subjunctive mood that
would yield "would," but the translation reflects the resolve to do
what is still at the moment contrary to fact. Thus the recognition may
evoke an intention to intervene in order to change the situation. The
subjunctive of recognition is voiced in verses 4–5a. Then comes the
imperative of action:

> You shall repay the principal amount and shall add one-fifth to it.
> You shall pay it to its owner when you realize your guilt. (v. 5b)

The required action is expressed in three verbs. The first, "repay,"
is *shalem*, a regular form for retribution that is linked to the familiar
noun *shalom*, thus shalom-making. The second verb, "add,"
concerns a requirement, perhaps a fine, whereby more is given
back to the neighbor than has been taken from the neighbor. The
additional 20 percent is a standard amount that is required in a series
of practices related to redemption (see Lev. 5:16; 27:13, 15, 27, 31;
Num. 5:7; in Gen. 47:24 it is the measure of rent paid to Pharaoh by
sharecroppers). The 20 percent is clearly a significant amount of cash
for an economic transaction added to the principal, in our case no
doubt to underscore the gravity of the affront, a significant amount
to dramatize in a face-to-face culture, a visible gesture indicating
serious reparation that entails both economic cost and social face.
The payment is a clear, public announcement of a violation, an
intentional act to move beyond the violation. In a word, this is *an act
of reparation* that constitutes the first step in reconciliation.

It is, however, of immense importance that this pivotal text on
overcoming sin does not stop with neighborly reparations. If the
sin were only against the neighbor, reparations might suffice. But
the affront is "a trespass *against the* LORD." Thus, after reparation

toward the neighbor, there remains the affront against YHWH that is constituted through the economic violation of the neighbor. For this, more is required, which can be affected only through the priest:

> And you shall bring to the priest, as your guilt offering to the LORD, a ram without blemish from the flock, or its equivalent, for a guilt offering. The priest shall make atonement on your behalf before the LORD, and you shall be forgiven for any of the things that one may do and incur guilt thereby. (Lev. 6:6–7)

The offering to be given is a "ram without blemish" or an equivalent, an animal of immense value in an agricultural economy. Such an animal is the best, the most expensive that can be offered. This particular priestly manual skips over the detail of slaughter and sacrifice, and characteristically offers no interpretation of the meaning of the act concerning how or why the offering of an animal accomplishes reconciliation. The priests seem committed to the proposition that the act—without any "theory of atonement"—accomplishes what must be accomplished in the broken relationship with the Lord. Thus the conclusion in verse 7 is that the priest "makes atonement," that is, accomplishes reconciliation. The outcome is forgiveness. The point that strikes me as important is that the priest effects the reconciliation, something the penitent cannot do for himself/herself. I judge that the priest is essential because the transaction is essentially *a sacramental one* that depends upon a credible, sustainable communal world of symbolization in which the guilty party is willing to participate by offering a costly contribution that becomes a vehicle and sign of moving past the affront against the Lord.

## III

I suggest that we can learn something important by considering an interface between the two texts in Matthew 5:23–24 and Leviticus 6:1–7. The priestly construction of Leviticus 6:1–7 consists in two actions, *a neighborly reparation* and *a sacramental submission* to the mystery of divine forgiveness. Both acts in turn are expensive, first repayment plus 20 percent to the neighbor, and then a flawless male ram, upon which the future of the flock depends. The teaching of Jesus in Matthew 5:23–24 does not correlate precisely with the text of Leviticus, even though it is clearly reminiscent of it. In Matthew the circumstance, not unlike that of Leviticus 6:2–3, is one of alienation, when "your brother or sister has something against you," that is, the brother or sister has been affronted. The cause of alienation is not as specific here, but the critical remedy is parallel: First, be reconciled to your brother or sister. The verb "be reconciled" is not inflected or exposited at all, but one may imagine that the act of reconciliation requires a substantive gesture of some kind, perhaps a verbal sign of apology and/or abasement, or perhaps a more substantive gesture commensurate with the substantive nature of the affront. One may imagine that the requirement constitutes something of a serious act of submission to the wronged brother or sister, more than a generic gesture, found adequate in a therapeutic society. Again, the act is one of reparation that is indispensable for reconciliation.

With that act completed, one may approach the altar with a gift. To be sure, this teaching of Jesus is not directly about "atonement," nor is the gift identified as a "guilt offering." Only two things are clear. First, the reconciliation remains incomplete without an approach to the altar, suggesting that more is entailed in forgiveness than simply a transaction with the neighbor. Second, an approach to the altar is not empty-handed, but with a gift that signifies a personal, serious engagement in approach to the place of Presence. It takes no stretch of imagination to see that in this teaching, like that of Leviticus, two acts are required in sequence, neighborly reparation and sacramental submission, both requirements entailing giving something of self away in acts of divestment and gestures of vulnerability.

## IV

It is worth noting that neither text offers any theory of atonement or any explanation about how restoration of relationship is accomplished. Nor does the text tell against a theology of unconditional grace, for it is an act of grace that God has provided these means for restoration, the means of *the altar* and its sacramental capacity and, derivatively, the means of *the text* that guides, also a gift of grace.

The *altar* and *text*, *sacrament* and *word*, are both gifts of God for the completion of the tasks of the reception of God's forgiveness.

Grace offered by sacramental and textual means must be actively received, in both cases by costly gestures toward God and toward neighbor. It occurs to me that by focus upon the two steps in both texts (*reparation* and *sacramental submission*), this twofold requirement correlates with the work of the Truth and Reconciliation Commission in South Africa. However that title for the commission came about, the phrasing is a mouthful of evangelical theology. The phrase recognizes a two-step process of reconciliation and understands how it is that the two steps are in sequence. The Truth and Reconciliation Commission is easily criticized for being inadequate in many ways. Its enactment was, nonetheless, in an arena of remembered violence and irreconcilable resentment and alienation of a most powerful kind. The task of the commission concerned the revivification of society in the midst of a real life-and-death struggle—nothing pretty.

The first step in such reconciliation is *truth*. The truth must be told about a violation of neighbor, and every "violation" perforce participates in *violence*. The truth must be told about violence perpetrated by one neighbor against another. In Leviticus 6, the violence is economic; in Matthew 5, the affront is unnamed, simply "something against you." The violence must be named and owned; gestures of compensation, remorse, and reconciliation for an alternative must be articulated, perhaps verbally, perhaps concretely in monetary terms. The overcoming of alienation is not cheap or easy, but requires truth-telling whereby the offender is placed at the behest of the offended in some concrete way.

Only when *truth* is told, can approach be made to the altar of atonement, that is, to the place of reconciliation. Reconciliation is finally not in the hands of the neighbor. It is in the hands of the priest (explicitly in Lev. 6, surely implied in the "altar" of Matt. 5), the one charged with nurturing and practicing the most elemental signs of holiness to which the community attests. The priest in both cases, on behalf of the present holy but unseen God, receives the gift, something of value. Of course, in such a transaction there are risks of bribery and reciprocity and even Anselm's notion of "satisfaction." The gift must nonetheless be offered as a gesture of submission, divestment, and vulnerability, the ceding over of one's life

to the mysterious worship of God's holiness. In sacramental awareness, we do indeed leave the altar differently, for the altar constitutes
an arena for the transaction of "transubstantiation" that is better left
unexplained, because more happens than can be explained.


# V


As I thought about these two texts, the condition of our society, and
the pastoral office, it occurred to me that we live in a social context where guilt and therefore forgiveness have been trivialized to be
irrelevant, whether it is a matter of rote repetition of "confession of
sin" and "assurance of pardon," or whether it is a mumbled whisper
of embarrassment.

We live in a society that is deeply alienated; but we also live
where the church and its pastors have been entrusted with the awesome, grace-given vehicles of restoration. The recovery of pastoral
practices of reconciliation might include the two steps outlined by
the priests that are echoed by Jesus:

1. *Truth-telling reparation toward affronted neighbor*, a truth-
   telling that might be concerned with large, public alienations, or
   it might be so concrete as alienations within families or congregations. The church may indeed be the arena for truth-telling that
   does not grovel in guilt but that readily undertakes the first step
   in reconciliation.
2. *Sacramental reconciliation* that requires a priestly enactment of
   divine reception of costly self-submission and a rendered verdict
   that the gift is adequate—made adequate by the gracious God
   who receives.

On this latter point, I have pondered pastoral authority. I am of
course aware of the abusive misfortune of the old priestly notion
of "absolution" that is an affront to evangelical Christians. That old
priestly practice smacked of authoritarianism and a hint of two-tiered
notion of church, of first-rate priests and second-rate laity. In place
of that practice, however, we have largely forfeited the priestly performative act of reconciliation that, I have no doubt, requires a for-
mal priestly utterance done with gravitas commensurate to our ocean

of alienation and appropriate to the new life that is born in, with, and under priestly utterance. A general good feeling or a therapeutic affirmation is no adequate substitute for a priestly performative verdict about the willingness of God to receive our submitted, divested, vulnerable selves.

## VI

The dramatic capacity of the church and its pastors in this regard is an astonishing, wondrous counterforce to the world of alienation that is all around us. There is, moreover, no other way to have the vicious cycles broken, and therefore we endlessly repeat the patterns of alienation that inevitably culminate in deathliness. My son John teaches in a fairly typical college social science department. He has observed over time that in every departmental meeting, all the old hurts and alienations are endlessly reiterated among colleagues. (I myself have seen traces of such faculty transactions in a somewhat different venue.) John, no mean theologian, observed: "The endless reiteration of such pain is because . . . they have no way to break the cycles of anger." What an insight so pertinent to our society!

Entertain that the church has entrusted to it by God the means of grace—*neighborly reparations* and *sacramental submissiveness*—that can break vicious cycles of alienation and make restoration to life possible. That evangelical reality is of course an embarrassment in a society where *truth* is rarely told and *reconciliation* is most often cheap and surface. The enactment of such an alternative is at the core of our faith, however it is that we speak of "atonement." At the center of such activity is the pastor, who has more entrusted in the pastoral office than we usually notice. If we were more self-aware of what belongs to the pastoral office, then we might recognize that what we do in the pastoral office is to conduct and enact myriads of Truth and Reconciliation Commissions. Such commissions occur randomly here and there; they have their primal locus in the weekly liturgy of forgiveness, where all of the grace of our Lord Jesus Christ and where all of the needfulness of God's people are dramatized, and where the fullness of God's grace is made available. In that centered environment of grace and gratitude, *neighborly reparation* and *sacramental submission* make sense, as they make sense nowhere else. The enactment of such Truth and Reconciliation Commissions may be the most important "social action" that we can undertake!

## Questions for Reflection

1. What examples (economic and otherwise) come to mind as you consider the link between transgressions against God and affronts against neighbor? What might reparations for those neighbors look like today?

2. Can you think of any examples from your life or from history in which a broken relationship was restored when an offending person both honestly named the offense and made substantive gestures of submission, divestment, and vulnerability toward the affronted neighbor and perhaps also toward God?

3. How might truth-telling reparation and sacramental reconciliation be recovered and expressed in your congregation's worship?

4. How has your understanding of God's grace grown as you have read this book?

# Acknowledgments

*T*hese pages constitute a continuation of the copyright page. Grateful acknowledgment is given to the following for permission to quote from copyrighted material by Walter Brueggemann:

Chapters 1 and 2 include revised material from Walter Brueggemann, "Food Fight," *Word and World* 33 (2013): 319–40, originally offered as the Heck Lectures at United Theological Seminary in Dayton, Ohio, in May 2011. Used by permission.

Chapter 3 includes revised material from Walter Brueggemann, "To Whom Does the Land Belong? 2 Samuel 3:12," *Journal for Preachers* 30 (2007): 28–35. Used by permission.

Chapter 4 includes revised material from Walter Brueggemann, "The Practice of Homefulness," *Journal for Preachers* 15 (1994): 7–22. Used by permission.

Chapter 5 includes revised material from Walter Brueggemann, "Cadences Which Redescribe: Speech among Exiles," *Journal for Preachers* 17 (1994): 10–17. Used by permission.

Chapter 6 includes revised material from Walter Brueggemann, "Sabbath as Alternative," *Word and World* 36 (2016): 247–56. Used by permission.

Chapter 7 includes revised material from Walter Brueggemann, *From Whom No Secrets Are Hid: Introducing the Psalms*, ed. Brent A. Strawn (Louisville, KY: Westminster John Knox, 2014). Used by permission.

Chapter 8 includes revised material from Walter Brueggemann, "Ministry Among: The Power of Blessing," *Journal for Preachers* 22 (1999): 21–29. Used by permission.

Chapter 9 includes revised material from Walter Brueggemann, "The Impossible Possibility of Forgiveness," *Journal for Preachers* 38 (2015): 8–17. Used by permission.

Chapter 10 includes revised material from Walter Brueggemann, "A Myriad of 'Truth and Reconciliation' Commissions," *Journal for Preachers* 28 (2005): 3–9. Used by permission.

# Notes

EDITOR'S INTRODUCTION

1. On this text and the many other passages in which it appears, sometimes as a quotation and sometimes reformulated in different ways, see Walter Brueggemann, *Theology of the Old Testament: Testimony, Dispute, Advocacy* (Minneapolis: Fortress, 1997), 215–28, and the sources cited therein.

2. See, for example, Phyllis Trible, *God and the Rhetoric of Sexuality* (Philadelphia: Fortress, 1978), 1–30; Michael Fishbane, *Biblical Interpretation in Ancient Israel* (Oxford: Clarendon, 1985), 341–50; and Thomas B. Dozeman, "Innerbiblical Interpretation of Yahweh's Gracious and Compassionate Character," *Journal of Biblical Literature* 108 (1989): 207–23.

3. Brueggemann, *Theology of the Old Testament*, 215.

4. See Brent A. Strawn, "YHWH's Poesie: The *Gnadenformel* (Exodus 34:6b–7), the Book of Exodus, and Beyond," in *Biblical Poetry and the Art of Close Reading*, ed. J. Blake Couey and Elaine T. James (Cambridge: Cambridge University Press, 2018), 237–56.

5. For a broader and longer discussion of these dynamics of scarcity and abundance in capitalism, see Todd McGowan, *Capitalism and Desire: The Psychic Cost of Free Markets* (New York: Columbia University Press, 2016), 197–214.

CHAPTER 1: FOOD FIGHT I

1. Abraham Maslow is often credited as the person who did the most to draw our attention to the connections among these several needs; see *Motivation and Personality* (New York: Harper, 1954). But, of course, demonstrations of such connections and tensions recur throughout Freud's work. For example, in "Civilization and Its Discontents," in *The Standard Edition of the Complete Psychological Works of Sigmund Freud*, vol. 21, trans. James Strachey (London: Hogarth, 1957), Freud claims that social reality—civilization—and the subjective ego are historical emergences out of id-level needs and desires. He even refers to various cultural advances as "prosthetic gods" (91–92).

2. Leon R. Kass, *The Beginning of Wisdom: Reading Genesis* (New York: Free Press, 2003), 569 and passim.

3. The note of "alas," here supplied from v. 1 even though it is not in the Hebrew of v. 4, is not a threat but a note of sadness, despite its traditional rendering as "woe." The poet speaks as if at a funeral, wanting to bring Israel to an acknowledgment of failure and danger. The address in v. 1 of "Zion" perhaps suggests the oracle was addressed to the south. Alternatively, the term "Zion" could refer to any group of urban elites, whether in the north or the south.

4. See John Donahue, *The Gospel in Parable* (Philadelphia: Fortress, 1988), 140. On the violation of food rules, see the difficult but rewarding discussion of Fernando Belo, *A Materialist Reading of the Gospel of Mark* (Maryknoll, NY: Orbis, 1981).

## CHAPTER 2: FOOD FIGHT II

1. See Walter Brueggemann, *An Unsettling God: The Heart of the Hebrew Bible* (Minneapolis: Fortress, 2009), 137–61.

2. See Walter Brueggemann, *Israel's Praise: Doxology against Idolatry and Ideology* (Philadelphia: Fortress, 1988).

3. See Michael Fishbane, *Sacred Attunement: A Jewish Theology* (Chicago: University of Chicago Press, 2008), and Judith Shulevitz, *The Sabbath World: Glimpses of a Different Order of Time* (New York: Random House, 2010).

4. See Sharon H. Ringe, *Jesus, Liberation, and the Biblical Jubilee: Images for Ethics and Christology*, Overtures to Biblical Theology (Philadelphia: Fortress, 1985).

## CHAPTER 3: TO WHOM DOES THE LAND BELONG?

1. J. Paul Getty once cynically remarked, "The meek shall inherit the earth, but that does not say anything about mineral rights under the earth."

2. It was Claus Westermann, in *What Does the Old Testament Say about God?* (Atlanta: John Knox, 1979), who first summoned Old Testament studies back to these issues by observing that the God who "saves" is the God who "blesses."

3. See a classic statement by C. B. McPherson, *The Political Theory of Possessive Individualism: Hobbes to Locke* (Oxford: Oxford University Press, 1962).

4. Lynn White Jr., "The Historical Roots of Our Ecological Crisis," *Science* 155 (1967): 1203–7.

5. See Cameron Wybrow, *The Bible, Baconianism, and Mastery over Nature: The Old Testament and Its Modern Misreading*, American University Studies Series 7, vol. 112 (New York: Peter Lang, 1991). Wybrow has effectively answered the charges of White.

6. See the discussions of the theological crisis of the Enlightenment by Paul Hazard, *The European Mind: The Critical Years, 1680–1715* (New York: Fordham University Press, 1990), and Stephen Toulmin, *Cosmopolis: The Hidden Agenda of Modernity* (New York: The Free Press, 1990).

7. Reference may also be made to the narrative concerning Jeremiah's ancestral rootage in Jer. 32. That narrative in Jeremiah betokens the inalienable right of the exilic community to the land of Israel.

8. Reference to this process is the center of the many writings of Wendell Berry, as for example, *The Gift of Good Land: Further Essays Cultural and Agricultural* (San Francisco: North Point Press, 1981). Berry's novel *Jayber Crow: A Novel* (Washington: Counterpoint, 2000) is an account of the loss of ancestral land in the face of aggressive acquisitiveness.

9. Most remarkably the catalog of sins in Col. 3:5 concludes "greed (which is idolatry)." In this phrasing the writer gathers together the first commandment and the tenth, and indicates that it is in economic transactions that false gods are embraced and practiced.

## CHAPTER 4: THE PRACTICE OF HOMEFULNESS

1. See Phyllis Trible, *God and the Rhetoric of Sexuality*, Overtures to Biblical Theology (Philadelphia: Fortress, 1978), 31–59.

2. See, e.g., Norman K. Gottwald, *The Tribes of Yahweh* (Maryknoll, NY: Orbis, 1979); Norman K. Gottwald, ed., *Social Scientific Criticism of the Hebrew Bible and Its Social World: The Israelite Monarchy* (Decatur, GA: Scholars Press, 1986); and Frank S. Frick, *The Formation of the State in Ancient Israel*, The Social World of Biblical Antiquity Series 4 (Sheffield: JSOT, 1985).

3. See the discussion of this text by José Miranda, *Marx and the Bible: A Critique of the Philosophy of Oppression* (Maryknoll, NY: Orbis, 1974), 47–72.

4. It is of course the case that the refraction of that early vision in the tradition of Deuteronomy is formulated much later. Nonetheless, the passions that drive the tradition are rooted in the faith and social experience of the origins of Israel. On critical questions related to Deuteronomy, see Patrick D. Miller Jr., *Deuteronomy*, Interpretation (Louisville, KY: Westminster John Knox, 1990).

5. I am following the hypothesis of a "peasant revolt" proposed by George E. Mendenhall and carefully pursued by Norman Gottwald and others. That hypothesis makes the most sense out of the violent destructions through which the promises of God were fulfilled to land-hungry Israel.

6. D. N. Premnath, "Latifundialization and Isaiah 5:8–10," *Journal for the Study of the Old Testament* 40 (1988): 49–60. See also John Andrew Dearman, *Property Rights in the Eighth-Century Prophets: The Conflict and Its Background*, SBL Dissertation Series 106 (Atlanta: Scholars Press, 1988). Wendell Berry, *A Place on Earth* (San Francisco: North Point Press, 1983), has written gracefully and positively about the ordering of a community with safe land in which everyone is "placed" with dignity and well-being. Moreover, he has done so without a tinge of the romantic.

7. Perhaps the man in the parable of Luke 12:16–20 is the concrete embodiment of this oracle. This man lives for coveting, celebrates alone, and dies in his foolishness.

8. On such a social analysis in relation to this text, see Hans Walter Wolff, "Micah the Moreshite—The Prophet and His Background," in *Israelite Wisdom: Theological and Literary Essays in Honor of Samuel Terrien*, ed. John G. Gammie et al. (Missoula, MT: Scholars Press, 1978), 77–84, and his citation of the programmatic work of Albrecht Alt in note 9.

9. This text, along with Ezek. 34:11–16, lies behind the great judgment scene in Matt. 25, which brings so close together God's own person and the reality of the needy.

10. The phrase is of course from Julian of Norwich (*Showings* [New York: Paulist, 1978], 225 and passim). Julian's usage is of course very different, but I cite it to suggest the linkage between spiritual well-being and material justice. It is the hope of prophetic faith that *all* will be well.

11. John H. Elliott, *A Home for the Homeless: A Sociological Exegesis of I Peter, Its Situation and Strategy, with a New Introduction*, repr. (Eugene, OR: Wipf & Stock, 2005 [1990]). On the "household" as a focus of early Christianity, see M. Douglas Meeks, *God the Economist: The Doctrine of God and Political Economy* (Minneapolis: Fortress, 1989), and the splendid study of the Gospel of Matthew by Michael H. Crosby, *House of Disciples: Church, Economics, and Justice in Matthew*, repr. (Eugene, OR: Wipf & Stock, 2004 [1988]).

12. On the widow, see Paula S. Hiebert, "'Whence Shall Help Come to Me?' The Biblical Widow," in *Gender and Difference in Ancient Israel*, ed. Peggy L. Day (Minneapolis: Fortress, 1989), 125–41. It is fair to translate from widow to orphan in terms of social analysis because the two shared the same jeopardy and vulnerability in tribal society.

13. On the social, spiritual dimension of homelessness, see Peter Berger et al., *The Homeless Mind: Modernization and Consciousness* (New York: Vintage, 1973).

## CHAPTER 5: CADENCES THAT REDESCRIBE

1. On my understanding of exile as a useful metaphor for the contemporary crisis of the US church, see Walter Brueggemann, *Cadences of Home: Preaching among Exiles* (Louisville, KY: Westminster John Knox, 1997).

2. Alan Mintz, *Hurban: Responses to Catastrophe in Hebrew Literature* (New York: Columbia University Press, 1984), x. I am indebted to Tod Linafelt for this most remarkable reference.

3. Mintz, *Hurban*, 2, italics added.

4. Paul Ricoeur, "Biblical Hermeneutics," *Semeia* 4 (1975): 107–45.

5. The "odd speech" with which Ricoeur deals includes proclamatory sayings, proverbs, and parables. See "Biblical Hermeneutics," 109–18.

6. Ricoeur, "Biblical Hermeneutics," 31, 127, and passim.

7. On lamentation, see Claus Westermann, *Praise and Lament in the Psalms* (Atlanta: John Knox, 1981).

8. See Mintz, *Hurban*, 17–48, for a suggestive discussion of Lamentations.

9. Mintz discerns what is at stake in this particular imagery: "The serviceableness of the image of Jerusalem as an abandoned fallen woman lies in the precise register of pain it articulates. An image of death would have purveyed the false comfort of finality; the dead have finished with suffering, and their agony can be evoked only in retrospect. The raped and defiled woman who survives, on the other hand, is a living witness to a pain that knows no release. It is similarly the perpetualness of

her situation that comes through most forcefully when Zion is pictured as a woman crying bitterly alone in the night with tears wetting her face (Lamentations 1:2). The cry seems to ululate permanently in the night; the tear forever falls to the cheek. It is a matter not just of lingering suffering but of continuing exposure to victimization" (*Hurban*, 24).

10. The contrast between the book of Lamentations and Ps. 74 is the difference between "lament" and "complaint." Erhard Gerstenberger, "Jeremiah's Complaints: Observations on Jer. 15:10–21," *Journal of Biblical Literature* 82 (1963): 393–408, draws the distinction nicely: "A lament bemoans a tragedy which cannot be reversed, while a complaint entreats God for help in the midst of tribulation" (405n50).The distinction and interrelatedness of the two are nicely expressed in German: *Klage* and *Anklage*.

11. On the cruciality of coming to speech, see Elaine Scarry, *The Body in Pain: The Making and Unmaking of the World* (New York: Oxford University Press, 1985), and Judith Lewis Herman, *Trauma and Recovery: The Aftermath of Violence—From Domestic Abuse to Political Terror* (New York: Basic Books, 1992).

12. The most complete study of the genre is by Edgar W. Conrad, *Fear Not Warrior: A Study of 'al tira' Pericopes in the Hebrew Scriptures*, Brown Judaic Studies 75 (Chico, CA: Scholars Press, 1985).

13. Joseph Sittler, *Grace and Gravity: Reflections and Provocations* (Minneapolis: Augsburg, 1986), 99–100. See the more comprehensive discussion by Gail R. O'Day, "Toward a Biblical Theology of Preaching," in *Listening to the Word: Studies in Honor of Fred B. Craddock*, ed. Gail R. O'Day and Thomas G. Long (Nashville: Abingdon, 1993), 17–32.

14. On this text, see Walter Brueggemann, "A Shattered Transcendence? Exile and Restoration," in *Biblical Theology: Problems and Prospects*, ed. Steven J. Kraftchick et al. (Nashville: Abingdon, 1995), 169–82.

15. I name economics and sexuality because these are the twin issues that vex and will continue to vex the church. It will be helpful to see that the two are deeply interrelated, as the parallel criticisms of Marx and Freud make clear.

16. See Walter Brueggemann, *Our Hearts Wait: Worshiping through Praise and Lament in the Psalms*, Walter Brueggemann Library, vol. 2 (Louisville, KY: Westminster John Knox, 2022), 65–86.

17. See the helpful discussion of this passage by Norbert Lohfink, *The Covenant Never Revoked: Biblical Reflections on Christian-Jewish Dialogue* (New York: Paulist, 1991), 45–57. Lohfink makes clear that the text cannot be interpreted in a Christian, supersessionist way.

18. On "forgiveness," see especially the exilic text of 1 Kgs. 8:27–53.

19. On the practice of promise among exiles in order to fight off despair, see Rubem A. Alves, *Tomorrow's Child: Imagination, Creativity, and the Rebirth of Culture* (New York: Harper & Row, 1972), 182–205. Alves writes: "Why is it so important to go on hoping? Because without hope one will be either dissolved in the existing state of things or devoured by insanity" (193).

20. My use of the term "end" here as a sense of terrible loss is intended to counter the argument of Francis Fukuyama, *The End of History and the Last Man* (New York: The Free Press, 1992). In my judgment his self-serving argument, that is, self-serving for Western capitalism, is a romantic fantasy. He understands the current "end" to be one of triumph.

21. Mintz, *Hurban*, 29.

## CHAPTER 6: SABBATH AS ALTERNATIVE

1. The themes of this chapter are more fully exposited in my book *Sabbath as Resistance: Saying NO to the Culture of Now* (Louisville, KY: Westminster John Knox, 2014).

2. Patrick D. Miller Jr., "The Human Sabbath: A Study in Deuteronomic Theology," *Princeton Seminary Bulletin* 6, no. 2 (1985): 81–97. In *The Ten Commandments* (Louisville, KY: Westminster John Knox, 2009), 117–66, Miller has provided the finest critical exposition of the Sabbath that we have.

3. See Joseph Blenkinsopp, "The Structure of P," *Catholic Biblical Quarterly* 38 (1976): 275–92, and P. J. Kearney, "Creation and Liturgy: The P Redaction of EX 25–40," *Zeitschrift für die alttestamentliche Wissenschaft* 89 (1977): 375–87.

4. See Jon D. Levenson, *Sinai & Zion: An Entry into the Jewish Bible* (New York: Winston, 1985), 111–37.

5. Michael Fishbane, *Sacred Attunement: A Jewish Theology* (Chicago: University of Chicago Press, 2008), 126.

6. See Frank Crüsemann, *The Torah: Theology and Social History of Old Testament Law* (Edinburgh: T. & T. Clark, 1996), 201–75.

7. See Walter Brueggemann, "The Countercommands of Sinai," in *Disruptive Grace: Reflections on God, Scripture, and the Church*, ed. Carolyn J. Sharp (Minneapolis: Fortress, 2011), 75–92.

8. Amartya Sen, *Poverty and Famines: An Essay on Entitlement and Deprivation* (Oxford: Clarendon, 1981), has forcefully contended that famine does not indicate an absence of food, but only a scarcity that drives up prices of food. The result is that the disadvantaged have no access to food that is indeed available for those with resources; see a case in point in 2 Kgs. 6:24–7:20.

9. Miller, "Human Sabbath," 93–97.

10. See Sharon H. Ringe, *Jesus, Liberation, and the Biblical Jubilee: Images for Ethics and Christology* (Philadelphia: Fortress, 1985).

11. See Marvin L. Chaney, *Peasants, Prophets, and Political Economy: The Hebrew Bible and Social Analysis* (Eugene, OR: Cascade, 2017), 67–82.

12. See Enrique Dussel, *Ethics of Liberation in the Age of Globalization and Exclusion* (Durham, NC: Duke University Press, 2013), on the perniciously negative dimensions of globalization.

## CHAPTER 7: DOXOLOGICAL ABANDONMENT

1. Karl Barth, *Wolfgang Amadeus Mozart* (Grand Rapids: Eerdmans, 1986), 37–38.

## CHAPTER 8: MINISTRY AMONG: THE POWER OF BLESSING

1. On blessing, see Claus Westermann, *Blessing in the Bible and the Life of the Church* (Philadelphia: Fortress, 1978), and Westermann, *Creation* (Philadelphia: Fortress, 1971).

2. The derivative blessing of humanity in Gen. 1:28 is clearly subordinate, as the man and the woman are a subset of creation. Attention should also be paid to Exod. 1:7, where it is Israel who "multiplies," thus embodying the blessings meant for creation. On the reiteration of the terms, see Walter Brueggemann, "The Kerygma of the Priestly Writers," *Zeitschrift für die alttestamentliche Wissenschaft* 84 (1972): 397–413.

3. See Gerhard von Rad, *Old Testament Theology*, vol. 1, *The Theology of the Historical Traditions*, trans. D. M. G. Stalker, Old Testament Library, repr. (Louisville, KY: Westminster John Knox, 2001 [1962]), 154–60.

4. Klaus Koch, "Is There a Doctrine of Retribution in the Old Testament?," in *Theodicy in the Old Testament*, ed. James L. Crenshaw (Philadelphia: Fortress, 1983), 57–87, has argued powerfully for *consequences* rather than divine intrusion.

5. See Hans Walter Wolff, "The Kerygma of the Yahwist," *Interpretation* 20 (1966): 131–58. Much of my argument here is derivative from Wolff.

6. The term "Canaanite" undoubtedly is not an ethnic term. It is rather a sociological, ideological term. Thus the Canaanites and the Israelites who polemicize against the Canaanites are in every respect exactly alike, except for the theological, ideological loyalties that distinguish them. The Canaanites are "neighbors" who are close at hand, but who confess different loyalties and so organize socioeconomic, political power differently.

7. Ps. 128 uses two different terms for "blessing." The term "happy" speaks of a more material, secular notion of blessing, whereas "blessed" in the latter verse is a more theological term. The two, however, are used together, thus bringing together the practical matter of material prosperity and the acknowledgment of YHWH as the God who blesses with prosperity. I should acknowledge that the valuing of children in the contemporary world is not in direct or full continuity with the ancient world, given the industrial revolution and the lesser economic need for children. Nonetheless, one may still notice: (a) in a nursing home the presence of a baby to touch and smell is indeed taken as a foundational sign of hope; (b) given all we know about birthing processes, it is still noteworthy that many couples desiring children go to great lengths, medically and economically, to secure children. The issues are not the same as in the ancient world. But they are not, in many cases, very different. A child is still in many ways the quintessential gift of the Creator.

8. See Claus Westermann, "Creation and History in the Old Testament," in *The Gospel and Human Destiny*, ed. Vilmos Vajta (Minneapolis: Augsburg, 1971), 11–38; and Westermann, *What Does the Old Testament Say about God?*, Sprunt Lectures (Atlanta: John Knox, 1979).

9. On the violence endemic in the text, see Regina M. Schwartz, *The Curse of Cain: The Violent Legacy of Monotheism* (Chicago: University of Chicago Press, 1997).

## CHAPTER 9: THE IMPOSSIBLE POSSIBILITY OF FORGIVENESS

1. The phrase is from the film *The Railway Man*; I have not read the book.

2. The classic statement is by Klaus Koch, "Is There a Doctrine of Retribution in the Old Testament?," in *Theodicy in the Old Testament*, ed. James L. Crenshaw (Philadelphia: Fortress, 1983), 57–87.

3. See Patrick D. Miller, *Sin and Judgment in the Prophets: A Stylistic and Theological Analysis* (Chico, CA: Scholars Press, 1982).

4. See Gerhard von Rad, *Wisdom in Israel*, trans. James D. Martin (Nashville: Abingdon, 1972), 124–37.

5. James Joyce is quoted by Richard Kearney, *Anatheism [Returning to God after God]* (New York: Columbia University Press, 2010). Kearny gives no specific citation.

6. Desmond Tutu and Mpho Tutu, *The Book of Forgiving: The Fourfold Path for Healing Ourselves and Our World* (New York: HarperOne, 2014), 218.

7. Walter Brueggemann, *The Psalms and the Life of Faith*, ed. Patrick D. Miller (Minneapolis: Fortress, 1995), 3–32.

## CHAPTER 10: A MYRIAD OF "TRUTH AND RECONCILIATION" COMMISSIONS

1. J. Louis Martyn, *Theological Issues in the Letters of Paul* (Nashville: Abingdon, 1997), 87.

www.ingramcontent.com/pod-product-compliance
Lightning Source LLC
LaVergne TN
LVHW021531060125
800513LV00015B/125